THE
COLOR
ANSWER BOOK

LEATRICE EISEMAN

THE
COLOR
ANSWER BOOK
From the World's Leading Color Expert

100+ Frequently Asked Questions for Home, Health and Happiness

LEATRICE EISEMAN
Executive Director, Pantone Color Institute
Director, Eiseman Center for Color Information & Training

CAPITAL
BOOKS, INC.
Sterling, Virginia

PHOTO: LLOYD FLANDERS

Copyright © 2003 by Leatrice Eiseman

All rights reserved. No part of this book may be reproduced or utilized in any form or by any means, electronic or mechanical, including photocopying, recording, or by any information storage and retrieval system, without permission in writing from the publisher. Inquiries should be addressed to:

Capital Books, Inc.
P.O. Box 605
Herndon, Virginia 20172-0605

References to PANTONE Colors displayed in this book, which are printed in four-color process, have not been evaluated by Pantone, Inc. for accuracy and may not match the PANTONE-identified standards. Pantone, Inc. assumes no responsibility for color inaccuracy. Consult current PANTONE Color Publications for accurate colors.

PANTONE®, PANTONE TEXTILE Color System® and the PANTONE Fan Chip Logo are the property of Pantone, Inc. Portions © Pantone, Inc., 2003.

Produced with the permission of Pantone, Inc. The PANTONE TEXTILE Color System® is a global system used to select, specify, communicate and control color in the apparel, home furnishings, architectural and interior design industries. It currently contains 1,925 fashion-forward textile colors dyed on fabric, each with its own unique PANTONE Number and name in six languages, and is continually updated. Over 200,000 textile professionals around the world use and rely on the PANTONE TEXTILE Color System®.

Cover photo: ©S. Dondicol
Half title page photo: John G. Hofland, Ltd.
Contents page photo: Vietri

ISBN 1-931868-25-5 (alk.paper)

Library of Congress Cataloging-in-Publication Data

Eiseman, Leatrice.
  The color answer book : from the world's leading color expert /Leatrice Eiseman.
      p. cm.
Includes index.
  ISBN 1-931868-25-5
  1. Color—Psychological aspects. I. Title.
  BF789.C7E375 2003
  155.9'1145—dc21
                          2003006694

Printed in Hong Kong.

First Edition

10 9 8 7 6 5 4 3 2 1

Also by Leatrice Eiseman

Alive with Color

The Pantone® Book of Color

Colors For Your Every Mood

Pantone® Guide to Communicating With Color

Contents

Acknowledgments

I want to thank all of the people who have contributed to this book. First, my accomplished, wonderful publisher and friend, Kathleen Hughes, who recognized the enormous need for books on color before anyone else in the publishing world did. She helped me tremendously with my very first book, again with my third book, and actually came up with the idea for this, my fifth book, *The Color Answer Book*.

A big thank you as well to Noel Grove and Barbara Payne who worked so diligently to get it all together and find many of the great images for the book, as well as Caroline Brock, the very talented art director. Of course, I owe a big debt of gratitude to the people who supplied the images, and they are all listed on the credit page.

With all of my worldwide travels and crazy schedule, I couldn't have completed this book without the help of my able assistant, Bobbie Hawkes. She truly has a "hawk-eye" for reshaping too-wordy sentences and a great eye for color.

My everlasting gratitude to good friends, family, and colleagues who have continued to encourage me in my work and in my quest for color questions, as well as my terrifically motivated seminar students who are always so open to learn more about the messages, meanings, and emotions of color.

I want to thank my friends and colleagues at Pantone, especially Lisa Herbert, executive vice-president, for help on this project as well.

And to my very supportive, ever-helpful husband, Herb, an expert in the music business, but whose favorite line is: "I taught her everything she knows about color."

PHOTO: GRANGE FURNITURE, INC.

Preface

Color is a catalyst for feelings—about how we look, decorate our home or office, plant in our garden, and relate to each other. The right colors stimulate or relax our senses, release happy memories, reflect how we feel about ourselves and our personal space.

With degrees and advanced studies in psychology and counseling, in addition to my background in business and color/design, I have traveled the world, answering questions about color. In my professional career as director of the Pantone Color Institute, seminar speaker, educator, media and color design consultant, manufacturers, businesses, and designers ask me how to make the best and most educated color choices for their products, packaging, corporate identity, and interior/exterior designs. Individuals ask me how color can make them look and feel better. I've answered literally thousands of such questions.

In these pages, I've selected the questions people ask me most and broken them into the areas that most affect our lives: emotional responses; wardrobe planning, makeup, hair color, and accessories; decorating home and office for ourselves and for those we live and work with; health; and gardening.

For most people, much of color "knowledge" is based on instinctive responses, cultural conditioning, and those aspects of color that we seem to absorb without much conscious thought. Yet there is a great deal we can learn about color that is based on certain artistic and harmonious concepts. These are the rules you'll learn in Chapter 1 that can make your use of color much more effective. Color theory informs us about various hues, their influence on each other, and ultimately, their influence on us.

We have learned that the response to color is a primitive one, often more emotional than intellectual. How people respond to color can give you some insight into their social orientation, their maturity (not always a good thing!), their cultural conditioning, self-esteem, and creativity. And it will also give you some clearer personal insights into all of the above.

Start with the color quiz in Chapter 2 to learn about your own emotional responses to particular colors and what your favorite (or least favorite) color says about you.

Color has a major impact on the way we see ourselves as well as on the way others view us. Color is so important in our perception of others that the first thing we see when someone approaches us from a distance is the color of his or her clothing. There are other clues, of course, such as verbal cues, body language, scents, and intuition; but the color of the clothing, as well as other body enhancement colors, has the most immediate effect. In Chapter 3, you'll find answers about clothes to make you look thinner, younger, sexier (if you need this information!), colors for your hair and makeup, stockings, shoes, and accessories (if you are a woman), and socks, shoes and ties for men. You'll also discover your best "signature" colors—those that are uniquely yours.

Shared space brings its own special color problems. Everyone has questions concerning the way family members relate and react to each other through color. Questions also arise regarding how family members react to the family pet, the family car, and special shared family occasions through color. Check out Chapter 4 to learn how color choices can bring on emotional family discord or harmony, depending on the situation.

Living in an age of alternative therapies, holistic remedies, and a newer, more enlightened view of nutrition, we seek to heal ourselves physically, mentally, emotionally, and spiritually. We strive to keep our bodies and psyches in balance. Color can be a powerful provider of guidance and insight for achieving that balance. Turn to Chapter 5 for the health-giving properties of color.

More than ever, our homes are critically important to our sense of comfort and well being. The act of decorating our homes is the catalyst that sparks our creativity, providing that special environment that helps us—and those we live with—thrive. Color is one of the most important elements in feathering our nests; and you'll find answers for decorating, redecorating, looking at color in relation to pattern and texture, and, most importantly, creating the best "color moods" in Chapter 6.

What about color in the workplace? Turn to Chapter 7 for a multitude of ways to use color in many phases of your professional and volunteer life, whether in a home office or a corporate cubicle. The most frequently asked questions are those regarding appropriate colors for a job interview, brightening up a boring space, or color as a means of communicating, and organizing business messages, as well as color in retail space.

Whether you have acres or a single pot to work with, nature offers a universe of colors to "paint" your outdoors beautiful. On that first spring day, when you stand in your garden, awed by nature and contemplating all that might be planted there, the choices can be overwhelming—which flowers, trees, and shrubs to plant; where to put each carefully chosen one; what to do first. This is where color really counts, as an organizing tool, as a mood-setter, as a way to be part of nature's grand scheme. Dip your trowel into Chapter 8 and get the "dirt" on how color can help you achieve your personal outdoor space.

Throughout the book, the color names that are capitalized and in bold face are from the PANTONE TEXTILE Color System®. I've used these color names because the PANTONE Color System is a global system used to select, specify, communicate and control color in the apparel, home furnishings, architectural, and interior design industries. Please use the Color Index in the back of this book for corresponding PANTONE Color names and/or numbers and for a brief description of the PANTONE Color shopping guide and where it may be obtained.

I hope that this book will bring you the answers you need, encourage you, enlighten you, and most of all, bring color into every aspect of your life.

—Leatrice Eiseman

PHOTO: CHICO'S RETAIL SERVICES, INC.

PHOTO: 18 KARAT INTERNATIONAL

PHOTO: DON PAULSON

CHAPTER ONE

Your Guide to Color Basics

There is a great deal we can learn about color that is based on certain artistic and harmonious concepts.

FOR MOST PEOPLE, much of color "knowledge" is based on instinctive responses, cultural conditioning, and those aspects of color that we seem to absorb without much conscious thought. Yet there is a great deal we can learn about color that is based on certain artistic and harmonious concepts. Although most people think of color in terms of objects or things that you can actually see, or imagine—a beautiful piece of glass, a glorious sunset, a great new shade of lipstick—color theory informs us about various hues, their influence on each other and, ultimately, their influence on us.

THE COLOR WHEEL

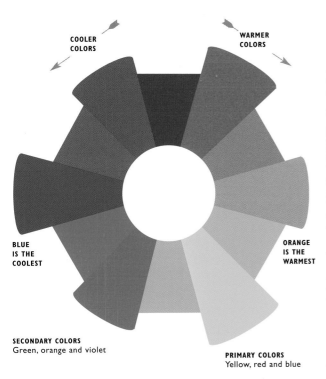

COOLER COLORS

WARMER COLORS

BLUE
IS THE
COOLEST

ORANGE
IS THE
WARMEST

SECONDARY COLORS
Green, orange and violet

PRIMARY COLORS
Yellow, red and blue

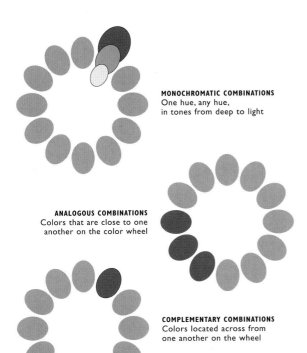

MONOCHROMATIC COMBINATIONS
One hue, any hue,
in tones from deep to light

ANALOGOUS COMBINATIONS
Colors that are close to one
another on the color wheel

COMPLEMENTARY COMBINATIONS
Colors located across from
one another on the wheel

1 What is the significance of the color wheel?

It's been said that the greatest of all inventions is the wheel. As an avid proponent of color I would say that the color wheel is next. Perhaps electricity, the cotton gin, and the internal combustion engine might be a bit more important for the advancement of industry, but the color wheel has certainly helped in the understanding and advancement of beauty. The color wheel is one of the most brilliantly conceived designs ever created as it graphically exhibits color relationships. When you learn to use the wheel to its full advantage, it can inspire a multitude of color combinations.

A quick review of the wheel (that you might have learned in grade school) shows that it originates with the three primary colors: red, blue, and yellow. Mix two of the primary pigments together and a secondary color results: orange (red and yellow), green (yellow and blue), and violet or purple (red and blue). Tertiary colors are created by mixing two secondary colors together. The colors are placed on the wheel, starting with red at the top and each color following in an orderly sequence.

Another basic concept illustrated by the color wheel is the perceived temperature of a hue. On one side of the wheel are the colors associated with heat or warmth: the advancing colors of fire, flame, and sparkling sun. On the other side of the wheel are the colors associated with cool: water, sky, forest, and the outer limits that seem to visually recede. However, changing an undertone can change the temperature. Blue reds are cooler than yellow reds. The redder the purple, the hotter it gets. Blue greens are cool, but the closer to yellow, the warmer green gets.

Complementary Colors
Study the colors immediately opposite each other. They are called complementary hues. Note that spelling is complementary with an "e" as they literally "complete" each other. Green is never greener than when it is positioned next to red. Yellow sparkles with

THIS BEAUTIFUL BOWL is an example of analogous colors. Adjacent hues on the color wheel will always blend since they are neighboring shades; and, just like all good neighbors, they are very compatible.

PHOTO: VIETRI

purple as its partner, and an orange sunset radiates more intensely against a deep blue backdrop. In the brightest intensities, these colors are completely opposite in character, making for interesting dramatic effects. Complementaries need not be the brightest version of each color family. They may be darkened, as in **Evergreen** against a **Scarlet** red or lightened, as in **Lily Green** paired with **Parfait Pink**.

Complementary colors can be used very effectively in interiors. A large painting with a **Sky Blue** background can be a perfect foil for a **Shell Coral** armoire. A wallcovering laced with leafy greens could be just the pick-me-up to the tired pink tiles in a once-bright bathroom. If a **Dark Denim** chair is fading in a bright sunny spot, a **Persimmon** pillow will help to revitalize it. If a **Celadon** green sofa is disappointingly dull, use something around it, on it, or under it that contains red, rose, or wine and watch it come alive again.

When graphic designers develop packaging for consumer products, they frequently use the brightest intensities of complementary colors. On your next trip to the market, look at the brilliant array of washing detergents all screaming for your attention and notice how many are done in the most blatant complementaries. Often this brilliant coloring is extended to the product itself, especially in the children's or 'tween market, as kids love brilliant complementaries such as neon pinky tones used with slimy greens.

Split Complementary Colors

A split complementary scheme uses a hue from one side of the color wheel with the two hues that lie on either side of the direct complement—for example, purple combined with yellow-orange and yellow-green. Although a description of this combination may seem a little garish, think about the many ways Mother Nature combines these shades in flowers. And she makes no mistakes!! Think of a **Bright Violet** flower with a Beeswax yellow center set against **Foliage** green. It is a visually stunning combination and not uncommon in flowers. The split complementaries may also be lightened, darkened, or muted for more subtle effects.

Analogous Colors

These are the colors that adjoin each other on the wheel. They are also referred to as neighboring or related colors that will happily combine. Refer to the color wheel on page 3 and imagine a combination of **Nasturtium** orange, **Sunset Gold**, and **Grenadine** red. To expand the family and add a hint of cool balance, use an adjoining yellow-green shade such as **Meadow Green**. To add some dramatic excitement to the combination, add a touch of **Meadow Violet**.

A wide range of lightness, darkness, and intensities can be used to offer more variety. Neutral tones may also be incorporated for variety. Another possibility to incorporate into the mix is a touch of a complementary color from across the wheel. An interesting aspect of analogous colors is that when a color needs to be "quieted," an adjacent analogous hue will tone it down. For example, **Vibrant Orange** in a print shirt will be less strident if a neighboring color such as **Pale Marigold** is included in the pattern.

Triads

A combination of three equidistant colors on the wheel of either primary or secondary colors creates a scheme of triads. They may be bright and spirited, as in the primary red, yellow, and blue, or in less saturated or deeper values of these colors, where the mood is more subtle. The secondary shades of orange, green, and purple might seem a bit "over the top" in the context of their brightest intensities; but again, when lightened, darkened, or grayed, these hues can create some very interesting and unusual combinations, especially when used in prints. An example of this kind of combination would be **Raspberry Wine**, **Deep Lake** blue interspersed with **Rich Gold** or **Almond Cream**, **Pastel Lilac**, and **Bermuda** green.

Tetrads

Two sets of complementaries used in a combination are called tetrads. This is a complicated challenge for the creative eye, but especially theatrical in more vibrant combinations. This is the kind of combination that can be found in exotic prints such as paisleys, ethnic-inspired motifs, which in turn offer up more choice in the way of accessories that will blend with the colors within the tetrad. When tetrads are used in lighter tints or midtones, they are more subtle, but no less effective, for example, **Peony** pink and **Malachite Green** or **Orchid** and **Golden Cream**.

2 What is the difference between color in pigments as opposed to color in lighting?

Those primary colors mentioned previously of red, blue, and yellow are not the same as the primaries used in lighting. Color in lighting is very different from color in pigments, such as dyes or paints. The primary colors of light are red, green, and blue-violet. They produce a secondary of yellow, which is obtained by adding red to green light; a mixture of red and blue light produces magenta, while blue and green light creates cyan. When all three primaries of light are mixed, they generate a white light.

The most beautiful example of color in light is the rainbow, that ever-fascinating visual phenomenon that always captures our undivided attention and astonishes our eyes with such vivid clarity. Each color in the rainbow has a different wavelength. Red has the longest wavelength and the slowest frequency, violet has the shortest wavelength and the fastest frequency.

Colored lighting is used most frequently in retail displays or for theatrical, architectural or landscaping effects. It can be especially effective in interior design when drama is desired. In recent years, supermarkets have discovered the effect of colored lighting, but it must be used with caution to create healthy effects when trained on food products. A blue turkey or green-tinted cheese would not be most consumers' idea of an appetizing food.

3

In your previous books, you refer to "crossover colors" and state that these are nature's most versatile colors. What are they and have you added any colors to the list?

In my first book, *Alive With Color*, I included 12 colors in a group that I called crossovers. These are colors that occur so frequently in natural settings that our eyes become accustomed to seeing them in combination with many other hues. They are nature's most versatile colors, and they enable us to go beyond the concept of typical neutral shades.

In a more recent book, *Colors For Your Every Mood*, **Teal**—another versatile and useable color, inspired by deep oceanic water colors—was added. In addition there are variations of neutral taupe, beige, and gray. This creates a total of 15 crossover colors.

Sky Blue

Have you ever seen a red rose, a purple crocus, or a yellow daisy against the backdrop of a clear blue sky and thought, "What a terrible combination?" Probably not. If we take the time to study the combinations in the context of how they are used in nature, we are more apt to be amazed at how some unlikely mixtures really do work. Blue skies, especially with their connotations of pleasant surroundings and promise of beautiful weather, provide the background for a multitude of nature's most ubiquitous colors.

How can you take advantage of Mother Nature's favorite background color? Hang a painting with blue sky as background in a room with a variety of colors; and, as our eyes are accustomed to sky blue as a backdrop, this color will not intrude on the surroundings. It is also an excellent way to bring a cool touch into a warm room to create color balance. (See color balance, Chapter 5, Question #9)

GREEN IS THE COLOR that is inevitably connected to nature and growth. As the background to all of the colors in the spectrum, green in its many variations is Mother Nature's most perfect neutral.

PHOTO: DON PAULSON

Pineneedle

Would you avoid placing a cascading ivy in the living room because it clashed with the carpet? Unless you have an absolute aversion to plants, the ever-present shades of greenery never seem invasive. When nature arranges flowers, green is the one color that appears in virtually every combination. Nature's greens are among the most versatile of hues, particularly shades of **Grass Green**, **Leaf Green**, **Forest Green**, and **Evergreen**. The great outdoors is filled with green foliage, trees, and grass. Even in the midst of silent snows, faithful pine trees soften the stark landscape with graceful green boughs.

Teal

The undulating color of a tropical sea, awash with both warm and cool currents, includes a variety of tones, from **Teal Green** to **Teal Blue**.

Sunlight Yellow

Give any child a box of crayons, and they invariably choose yellow to draw a big ball of sun (radiating with rays) in the upper left- or right-hand corner of the drawing. The universal concept of yellow as sunlight permeating the Earth's atmosphere contributes to the perception of yellow as a coordinating background or foreground color. It is a welcome sign of warmth and good cheer in a room full of cool colors.

Light Taupe and Bleached Sand

Ideal neutrals, these are variations of taupe and beige, the color of sand and stone. There is no end to the versatility of these balanced neutrals. They are wonderful when-in-doubt colors that work equally well with warm and cool undertones.

Neutral Gray and Pewter

Two more ideal neutrals, these shades of gray are the best "blenders." In the context of nature, gray appears subtly at dawn and dusk, often as an undertone to the blue sky or as the actual color of the sky when it is overcast.

Dark Earth

The varying Earth tones associated with rich soil, tree bark, and woodsy plants are an integral part of nature's basic color scheme. Your eye is accustomed to these unobtrusive colors, which function extremely well as neutrals. With so many people into gardening, "dirty" brown is now a good thing!!

Eggplant (Aubergine)

A perfect marriage of purple and maroon, and an interesting relief from deeper, more somber shades, Aubergine (the French word for eggplant) has become a classic.

Red Mahogany

Related to both **Deep Claret** and **Eggplant**, this elegant brown has a complexity that blends beautifully with many other colors.

True Red

Think about the frequency of red in nature and how it has been used as a signal color in natural settings. **True Red** is the most versatile of reds; it gives life to both warm and cool colors.

Deep Claret

These darker, delicious robust reds mimic the colors of the berries and grapes from which they are derived. They may range from deep wine shades such as **Ruby Wine** to **Malaga**, combining the mystery of purple with the deep richness of red and a splash of brown.

True Navy or Midnight Navy

The color of the sky as it descends into night, **True Navy** is associated with the strength and power of black, yet it is less mysterious. It is a familiar background color, and the most universal of all basic colors.

Raven

Just as night always follows day, black is the inevitable shade. Its protective cover brings both strength and power as humans are simultaneously comforted by the respite and cover of night, intrigued by the prospect of what the darkness might hold and fascinated by the mystery of its protective shroud. **Raven** is the quintessential basic color, offering a sophisticated backdrop to all other colors.

4 How do colors get their names?

I plead guilty to being one of those color namers, as I have identified and named literally thousands of colors. It sounds like fun and games and is, for the most part. But, trust me, when you have to name more than 50 at a time, the challenge can be daunting. For example, when working on a color-naming project for a paint company, I had the challenge of naming more than 2,500 colors.

I did have some help from various groups (yellow group, green group, red group, etc.) that were made up of professional colleagues, former students, creative friends, and family. My contribution was not only to oversee and name most of the colors, but also to check all names for accuracy and appropriateness. Finally, I needed to be absolutely certain that another color group had not used the name. In addition, the names could not be too trendy (rendering them dated in a short span of time), and the colors could not have been used previously in another system owned by the same company. You can get pretty silly or brain-dead at the end of a project like that, and I was both. As a result, some of those names never saw the side of a paint can: (Squished Caterpillar Green, Doo Doo Brown, Scarlet O'Haira & Red Butler, Nurple (a combo of navy and purple.)

I know there are some people (mostly left-brainers) who would prefer dropping the names and using a simple numerical system for all color. Personally, I like numbers for simple organizational identification, but for the romance, sizzle, mood, power of suggestion, and pure persuasion, there is nothing like a name.

Color names come from various sources, starting in ancient times to describe light and dark, day and night. Then came the association of color with various natural phenomena such as red with blood, yellow with sun, the green of vegetation, blue of sky and water, brown of the Earth, and the remaining colors that are also evident in the environment.

In some languages, such as the Shona language of Zimbabwe, no words exist to distinguish between red and orange, while in other cultures color names describe some pretty basic functions. In the Eskimo language, for example, blood and bile are used as descriptive words, as is the name for a purpled red, which literally means the color of a person who has choked to death!

For the most part, color is described with more aesthetically pleasing words. **Chinese Yellow** was adapted as a color name for this imperial shade, because the ancient Chinese venerated yellow as the color of the emperor and only he could wear it (talk about an exclusive club!). One ruler actually called himself the Yellow Emperor, and it is only fitting that a color was named in his honor as he is reputed to have been the inventor of Chinese script.

The name of a color draws our attention more forcefully to the attributes of a color. A color called **Chocolate Brown** is perceived of as delicious and rich, but **Decadent Chocolate** tempts us even more. **Champagne Beige**, as in plush carpeting, is seen as much more upscale than a nondescript beige. A lipstick called **Hibiscus** is far more suggestive of tropical delights than the unimaginative and uninspired "shade #10."

Here are some of the most inspirational sources and examples of color names:

Sources of Color Names

- Natural Phenomena: **Green Haze, Desert Dust, Storm Gray**
- Flowers, vegetation, and woods: **Primrose Yellow, Asparagus Green, Tawny Birch**
- Minerals, gemstones, and metals: **Amber Gold, Violet Quartz, Peridot, Medal Bronze**
- Animals, birds, and fish: **Sable, Dove, Bird of Paradise, Oyster Gray**
- Geography: **Coastal Fjord, Tibetan Red, Parisian Blue, Bordeaux**
- Foods, dyes, and spices: **Apricot Nectar, Chardonnay, Caramel Cream, Madder Brown, Ochre, Toasted Nut, Indigo, Curry**

Additional color terms spring from a flight of fancy or the fertile imagination of the colorist/designer/writer to depict a mood, paint a picture, and most of all—to entice.

- **Fiesta** (red) and **Confetti** (hot pink) radiate with excitement and fun.
- **Arabesque** (deep coral) combined with **Persian Violet** (blue violet) conjures up fantasies of Arabian Nights.
- **Ebony** (black) and vibrant **Ultra Violet** suggest sophisticated elegance.
- **Soothing Sea**, a clean, clear light blue-green, is instantly perceived as quiet, relaxing, and restorative.
- **Shocking Pink** informs us that this is not a color for a shrinking violet.

5

I am always confused by color terminology. What is the difference between tone and undertone, value, saturation, and all of those other confusing terms?

I can understand the confusion, so let's simplify the descriptors that will make it easier to recognize certain properties of color and help you to appreciate the many nuances of color. Besides, it's fun to learn to speak like a color "pro" and dazzle your friends with your knowledge. The most important words follow.

PAINTING: DEBORA HOUSE, "ANOTHER MOMENT IN TIME"

This evocative painting is a study in varying color values. While there are subtly related values above the horizon line, the contrast of light to dark values that meet at the horizon line brings a dramatic dimension to the turbulent waters.

- Hue: This is a synonym for the name of the color that reflects the dominant wavelength; for example red, blue, yellow, and so on.

- Saturation: Saturation or chroma describes the intensity of a color—how much or how little gray it contains. The purer a color, the more it approaches the colors of the spectrum, and the greater its saturation. So the word "saturation" means just that—the color can't be any "truer" than that. Colors at their highest chroma or saturation are at their ultimate brilliance, while lowered saturation makes them much more subdued and muted.

- Value: The lightness or darkness of a color is called its value. Closely related values are seen as calm and quiet, while sharp changes in value suggest more drama. The impact of color is not just about the actual hue, but also involves the saturation and value.

- Undertone: This denotes an underlying color within any given hue. For example, yellow in yellowish green, red in reddish violet, gray in grayish blue. Another word for undertone is cast, as in brown with a red cast.

- Tone: A mixture of a saturated color with gray.

- Shade: Although this word is often used interchangeably with the word color, a shade is actually a mixture of a fully saturated hue with black.

- Tint: A tint is a mixture of a saturated hue with white, so that pastels are all tints.

6

Are monotone color schemes the same as monochromatic?

Actually, they are very different and should not be used interchangeably. A monochromatic color scheme involves the use of one hue in varying tints, tones, shades, and intensities. If the hue family is blue, for example, the variations could range from the palest baby blue to the deepest recesses of royal blue. This kind of interplay between varying shades of the same family can be very dramatic. In this example, using the blue family, the monochromatic color scheme really gets the cooling, soothing psychological message of blue across to the viewer. Obviously, this could be very effective in packaging, on the printed page, or on a web page. It is also very effective in costuming or fashion illustration.

But in real-life situations, the effect can be overwhelming, especially if the brightest intensities of the color family are used in large amounts. For use in the home, monochromatic mixtures must contain enough contrast to help direct the eye to a focal point.

A monotone scheme describes the use of one single neutral in varying tints, tones, and shades. Taupe, off-whites, grays, and beiges are considered neutrals. Monochromatic tones are considered chromatic (with color) while neutrals are considered achromatic (without color). In actual usage, monotone schemes seldom remain purely neutral. An office in varying tones of beige may have a large window where the outdoor colors become a part of the vista. A pastel painting will bring color, no matter how subtle, to a pearl gray room. To keep monotones from becoming monotonous, a variety of textures, shapes, and contrasts needs to be combined.

When used in clothing, monotones are seldom absolutely neutral, because the personal coloring of the wearer provides contrast to the clothing. In signage, packaging, advertising, and other graphic applications monotones can disappear, or appear so subtle as to be unreadable, so it is necessary to use some strong contrast to gain attention.

7

I seem to have a good eye for color, but I still manage to make mistakes that I don't see until I get my purchase home. What am I doing wrong?

My first response is, "Nobody's perfect!" Even professionals make mistakes from time to time, although they might not admit it. Often the mistakes are brought about by influences over which you have no control, such as lighting. We all have suffered through the frustration of poor lighting in stores. We think the specific color is perfect in that setting and then take it outside or take it home only to find the color looks very different. In professional color parlance, this is called metamerism, where colors viewed under one set of conditions and lighting will mismatch when viewed under another.

There is not much we can do about poor or inadequate lighting in a store except to complain to the right people and make certain the item is returnable. If you can get the item into a clear, true daylight setting, all the better. But, in many retail settings, good luck on finding daylight anywhere. Some stores, especially paint outlets, are making an effort to correct the lighting problems and often offer special light boxes, used by professional colorists, to simulate various kinds of light sources.

House & Garden

MAKE THE MOST OF COLOR

49 WAYS TO USE COLOR IN YOUR ROOMS

**ADVANCE
RETAIL
TRADE
EDITION**

September 1951   50 Cents

COPYRIGHT 1951, THE CONDÉ NAST PUBLICATIONS INC.

PHOTO: HERBERT MATTER/HOUSE & GARDEN, © CONDE NAST PUBLICATIONS INC.

8

Do colors go in and out of style on a regular sequence?

It's more like an irregular sequence than a regular one. Many things can cause the revival of a color. However, the strongest revival of trends comes in 20- to 30-year cycles. This does not mean that the color will disappear entirely, banished by all designers and colorists within that time period. It may resurface for a short time span, most often in a fashion "moment" and be proclaimed in fashion magazines as the color of the season. Sometimes, the color catches on for more than a blip in time and spreads through many design disciplines.

In recent history, mauve emerged as the hottest color of the early 1980s. *Time Magazine* referred to the period as the "mauving" of America. Every doctor or dentist's office, hotel lobby, and living room carpet was some variation of mauve. It was used extensively in print, packaging, and posters as well. The ultimate compliment of the day (as invented by Billy Crystal) was the colorful comment: "You look mauvelous!"

The mass of 1980s mauve was precipitated by a prior decade of avocado—the dreaded "A" word. By the end of the 1970s everyone had been "avocadoed" to death. As a result, designers and colorists turned the color wheel around to the opposite side to search for the complementary colors. Although not the absolute complement to green, pinky purple, or purply pink, **Pale Mauve** was the perfect antidote to the overdone green.

Mauve was "in" for about six years, but as conspicuous consumption ruled the day, more vibrant colors were ushered in, and out went mauve. After 20 years had passed, it was inevitable that mauve would resurface in the early 2000s. Even the dreaded avocado made a comeback in the late 1990s, after an approximate 25-year hiatus. But it is now more apt to be combined in a far more delicious way, as in **Avocado** and **Sangria** red as opposed to **Avocado** and **Harvest Gold**.

Color trends can lead to color trouble. They can be exciting and novel, but run the risk of becoming passé very quickly. When a color story is new and popular, the market can become saturated with it. So, what may seem unique becomes a cliché if many people are using it in exactly the same way. It's the "new" color in combination with other established and/or basic colors that keeps the look fresh and personalized.

In apparel there is always a place for newness, especially in accessories. Bathrooms and bedrooms are good places for trend colors; it is less expensive to change towels and duvet covers than it is to recover a chair. Tabletop linens, pillows, and floral arrangements all provide relatively inexpensive opportunities to experiment with trend colors. It is part of the human condition to seek novelty. This can certainly be accomplished with a fresh "new" hue.

THIS COVER OF HOUSE & GARDEN magazine for September 1951 depicts the popular colors of that exuberant, optimistic Postwar era. Housewives were encouraged to use more color in their homes and everything was "looking up."

9 How and where do color trends start?

This is a question that intrigues everyone. Conventional wisdom has it that it all starts with fashion, and although that is not an absolute anymore, for the most part it is the fashion world that gives color trends a start. The color ball can get rolling with the textile designers/manufacturers who provide the color offerings in the fabrics, the designers/colorists who select or specify the fabrics as well as the color forecasters who provide color services and trend concepts to various industries.

So where do they get their ideas? First of all, it's not a divine inspirational lightning bolt that strikes from above. It takes a great deal of observation, reading, research, and discussion with people in various walks of life about trends in general that might not seem to have anything to do with color at all. It takes an open mind, curiosity, and a willingness to abandon personal prejudices about color and to look at color from a more universal standpoint.

As mentioned in the preceding question, timing is everything. If a color is introduced before its time, it can bring disaster in the marketplace to the designer, marketers, and manufacturers. But if the timing is right, consumers will be far more open to a specific color family.

For example, the green family got an unexpected push from the emergence of the environmental movement of the 1990s, continuing on well into the 2000s. Ecology was and still is on everyone's mind.

COLOR TRENDS TODAY, especially for the home, are no longer just about the one "hot" color that everyone must buy. Instead, there are integrated palettes of directional colors that offer a fresh, new, well-coordinated choice to today's more demanding and color-savvy consumer.

PHOTO: FIESTA® KEN MENGAY PHOTOGRAPHIC ILLUSTRATIONS

Companies today that are proactive and concerned about sustaining the environment are referred to as "green industries." So you can see how a color family connected to such an important social issue has the potential to become popular.

Green has gotten a bit of tweaking along the way; from **Pine Green** to **Peapod**, **Grass Green** to **Green Tea**, people today are far more open to the hue than ever before because of the special and important meanings that green represents.

Trends are always an important part of my color consulting work, so I always look at the following areas for major color trend influences:

FASHION: As previously mentioned, fashion is often a forerunner to colors that will eventually appear in other areas of design, especially as so many designers are now designing for the home as well.

THE ENTERTAINMENT WORLD: This is especially important in predicting directional colors for children's products. An appealing character of a particular color in an upcoming film or video game can influence many industries, such as toys, school supplies, and bed linens. Films have a longer shelf life, as eventually they become videos that are played over and over and over again! There are often sequels that eventually are released as videos. A beloved yellow-green Shrek not only brings the color into prominence, but also prolongs the life of the color. Television has also helped to disseminate or inspire trends through various home decorating shows and entire channels such as HGTV.

The music industry in the form of colors worn by popular stars in music videos or appearing on album covers can spawn a new color. Think of the Beatles' Yellow Submarine and other psychedelic album covers of the 1960s, the grungy garage rock band shades of the early 1990s, the glamorous and vibrant colors worn by today's "divas."

THE ART WORLD: With advance news of an upcoming collection, especially one that will travel to different venues, forecasters and designers take notice. Georgia O'Keefe's gorgeous southwestern desert colors helped to spawn the Santa Fe look, while Dale Chihuly's undulating designs in glowing colors have brought an enticing dimension to colored glass as inspiration for new color combinations.

CYCLICAL PATTERNS: Colors will always be recycled as they are often part of a designer's inspiration from the past. For example, in the waning years of the 1990s with the uncertain challenges of a new millennium—hopeful, yet at the same time anxious—nostalgic retro shades reappeared as people longed for the safer and sillier world of the "I Love Lucy" 1950s.

LIFESTYLES: Will casual blue denim continue to be the fabric of choice, or will more deeply hued formal looks hold sway? Will adrenaline-pumping sports activities that demand bright colors rule the day or will the survivor-type natural camouflage colors take charge? These might seem fashion-oriented issues, but they are eventually tied to color directions.

CULTURAL INFLUENCES: Color forecasts are often inspired by and spiced with a mixture of ethnic influences. Colors suggestive of various cultures, such as **Cayenne** or **Curry**, **Fandango Pink**, **Festival Fuchsia**, or exotic locales such as **Tropical Green** and **Inca Gold**, can all influence upcoming trends.

SOCIO-ECONOMIC ISSUES: The "socio" aspect of this question was answered previously with the symbolic usage of green and ecology, but as seemingly far removed as color may seem from an economic issue, it can be one of the most influential areas. Historically, when the economy is up, consumers (and designers) are apt to use the vital optimistic colors. When the economy is down, they are apt to play it safe. However, as there are many more "color converts" today than ever before because of many more resources such as shelter magazines, websites, and TV shows, it's difficult to imagine a time when the bland will again be leading the bland.

10

What do color professionals, such as designers, use to communicate color? Is there a "language" of color?

As you probably know, it is nearly impossible to remember a color accurately unless you have a sample of that color with you when you are trying to replicate it. When you are trying to combine colors, it is important to be as accurate as possible to see how well they blend with each other.

Some people have remarkable color memories, yet they are sometimes surprised at the fact that no matter how close they came to a perfect match in their "mind's eye," a little nuance of the color could be missing—a bit more green, a smidgen of yellow, just a bit brighter or duller and so on.

Professionals can't afford to be too far off as it is their job to get it right; and truly color-sensitive people, who may or may not be professionals, are never happy with near-misses. It will always bother them to look at the results of an almost-match, yet alone a glaring mistake.

Think of the designer in New York who must communicate the color she envisions on a garment to the person in India who is dyeing the fabric for the garment. Imagine an interior designer trying to explain his image of a carpet color without an accurate display of color examples. Of course, he could always haul around hundreds of carpet samples, but they still might not be what the client wants. That is where a color communication system that clearly shows a large array of colors, arranges them in color families, and provides a method of identifying those colors in a convenient format is so important.

The PANTONE Color language is the most universally understood standard available, providing color systems and leading technology for the selection and accurate communication of color. The PANTONE name is known worldwide as the standard language for color communication, from

WHETHER A PROFESSIONAL designer, manufacturer, colorist, or a consumer trying to decide how the living room wall will blend with the sofa and carpet, relying on color memory simply isn't always accurate. The most widely used systems for color selection, communication, and coordination are the color tools available from Pantone, Inc.

IMAGE PROVIDED COURTESY OF PANTONE,INC. © PANTONE INC., 2003

designer to manufacturer to retailer to customer. Pantone serves a wide array of industries, including graphic design, printing, publishing, textile, and plastics.

The PANTONE TEXTILE Color System® is available in printed form as well as textiles, and was developed to serve the needs of the home and commercial furnishings industries, as well as cosmetics and fashion. Many designers in those areas use this system to identify, communicate, and combine colors. Typically, a professional will use a fan guide to identify a color and has the option of pulling a paper chip (or a textile swatch) out of a book or file to affix to the design, color board, or collage.

Consumers who wish to use the tools traditionally available to professionals now have the option to purchase a paper guide similar to the one used by professionals. This can certainly alleviate the problem of dragging a big sofa pillow or bedspread to the store by simply identifying the closest color in the guide to the object that you are trying to coordinate.

Most of the color notations in this book come from the PANTONE Textile Color System®. However, one group of notations is drawn from the PANTONE MATCHING SYSTEM® as it addresses the use of color in the printing and graphics industry, specifically color use in stationery, business correspondence, cards, letterheads, and websites.

11 Are there any colors that are considered upscale or low-end?

From a historical perspective, an interesting aspect of "upper class" and "lower class" colors is that for many centuries, color was affordable only to the wealthy. Low-tech methods of obtaining dyes, such as the extrusion of mucous from the glands of tiny mollusks to render purple dye, were extremely labor intensive as it took 336,000 of the little critters to produce one ounce of dye! As a result of the expense involved, the poor wore rather colorless clothing. It wasn't until the Industrial Revolution that color was made available to the masses, at least in so-called "civilized" societies.

As was often the case, when color, or any other aspect of style and color, became available to the masses, the wealthy sought to disassociate themselves from those styles and colors. So the pendulum swings in color and design, just as it has in every other aspect of life.

Concepts of expensive color versus cheap changed enormously in the last decade of the 20th century. For example, for several decades of the mid-20th century, as a result of greater availability of less expensive household goods, vibrant orange was thought of as a cheap color. However, with the use of orange by high-end fashion designers, such as Versace, Hermes, Carolina Herrera, Oscar De La Renta, and Missoni, orange became less stigmatized. Abstract art, especially as it became more mainstream, also contributed to a greater sense of appreciation for vivid colors.

The concept of cheapness today is more often related to fabrication or to poor workmanship than to color. For example, synthetic fabric of poor quality in orange (and most other colors) would be perceived as cheap whereas orange in a lustrous silk or sumptuous velvet would not.

An intense purple such as **Bright Violet** was also thought of as tacky, as were **Bubblegum** pink or **Lime Punch**. But that was in the days of limited technology in mass-produced dyes and slick cheap-looking surface treatments, especially in plastics. Newer, more advanced technology enables even the cheapest plastic surfaces to look as if they are of higher quality.

Depending on where you were raised, the rules you were raised with, and your age group, you might still have a problem using those vibrant shades. Try to keep an open mind, as it is refreshing to experience something new in a color that you haven't tried before. Use these literally "stunning" colors in art, accessories, or in "fun stuff."

As to "high-end" image, as it is termed, neutrals and basic colors were recommended for more expensive products, clothing, or interiors because of their subtlety. The attitude was that there was no need to shout ostentatiously to command attention. As a result, "upscale" and "understated" neutrals and basics were associated with good taste. These classic shades are still considered tasteful, but today it is not necessary for so-called good taste to fade into the woodwork.

Again, with haute designers using hotter hues as well as the infusion of multi-cultural themes in art, advertising, packaging, fashion, and interiors, there is a greater appreciation and a greater diversity of all colors, so that the concept of cheap versus expensive is not as rigidly prescribed as in the past.

12 Is there truly a "psychology" of color?

There is no question that color wields a powerful psychological message. Indulge me for a moment and imagine a scenario where, having heard what you thought might be a prowler in the backyard, you called your local police department. They respond to your call, you open the door and there stand two policemen in **Lollipop** red uniforms, **Peacock Blue** polka dot ties, worn with **Sunny Lime** shirts and matching caps. You might be inclined to call the prowler in to protect you from the police!

Of course, this is a totally ludicrous example, as we know there would be no credibility suggested in this whimsical combination of cartoon character colors. They would look more like escaping circus clowns than benevolent protectors. They are far more likely to appear in deep **True Navy** pants, jacket, tie, and caps, denoting a dependable, strong, credible image, worn with a white shirt that speaks of purity and cleanliness.

Every color has a meaning that we have either learned by association or inherently sense that enables us to recognize the color message. For example, red is imbued in the human psyche as a call to action—an instinctively primal reaction as it is the color of blood and fire, two very important elements for human existence. They are, at the same time, life-threatening, yet life-sustaining.

When you were a little kid, Mommy or Daddy took your hand when you came to a stop sign at an intersection (or more likely pointed out the warning from the car) and said, "Red means stop." There are cultural and traditional meanings of colors as well as their broader associations as they appear in natural settings, such as a tranquil blue sky or a sunny yellow that is always perceived as warm.

We also have purely personal reactions to color that are most often based on childhood experiences:

- Those that made us very happy—a shiny new red bike as a birthday present

- Those that made us very sad—the color of the little brown squirrel that you ran over when you were speeding on that bike

- Those that were traumatizing—the color of a hospital's emergency room walls on the day you broke a leg and had to suffer through the anxiety

If you were on that red bike on the day you broke your leg, then red might not be one of your favorites, unless the happiness of getting that bike overrode the anxiety you felt at breaking your leg. As you can see, color reactions can be very personal, yet there are general messages that have been gleaned from research, including word association studies that do show some universality in feelings about specific colors.

You will have the opportunity to explore your own feelings about color when you take the word association color quiz in Chapter 2.

13 What is the color spectrum?

Sir Isaac Newton gave the world some astonishing information about color when he discovered the spectrum in 1666. He placed a wedge-shaped piece of glass, a prism, in a beam of white sunlight, which split into a radiating fan of seven hues—red, orange, yellow, green, blue, indigo, and violet. The spectrum is formed by waves of radiant energy from the sun that bend when they strike the prism. Each wave is a different length; red is the longest, gradually reducing in length to violet or purple as the shortest. The longest waves bend the least, while the shortest rays bend the most, so that the light comes out of the other side of the prism as separate waves.

Sir Isaac related the seven colors to the seven notes of an octave, which offended his scientific colleagues as they thought this perpetuated mystical nonsense. Interestingly, sound was later shown to affect the perception of color. Listening to high-pitched tones can make colors appear lighter, while low-pitched sounds tend to deepen color. Both the eye and the ear respond to waves of energy.

Newton created the first color wheel. Indigo is not included in the modern six-hued wheel as it becomes a gradation of the overlapping red and blue of the circle, ultimately forming violet or purple.

The color of an object will be visible only if this color is present in the source of illumination. Sunlight contains all the colors of the spectrum, while artificial lighting can be composed of these colors in varying amounts. Without natural or artificial light, there is no color.

14 How do we actually perceive color?

Contrary to what most people think, color is not actually the inherent property of an object. A leaf of spinach is not actually green, nor is a strawberry red. Instead, its color is dependent upon the absorption and reflection of light waves. As a result, color is the property of light that depends on wavelength.

When the light waves reach an object, some of the light is absorbed and some is reflected. Only the reflected light is seen by the eye. A spinach leaf appears green because it reflects only the waves producing the green light. The same holds true for the red strawberry or any other colored object.

The eye and the associated nerves register the reflected color on the retina, a light-sensitive membrane in the back of the eye containing rods and cones. The rods and cones define the color and the shape of the object by transforming the radiant energy into chemical energy, sending impulses to the optic nerve. The optic nerve registers the message and sends it to the control center—the brain. After this entire and rather complicated process, we become aware of the color of any given object.

That explains the physical phenomenon. However, color perception goes beyond the physical effects and ultimately includes the emotional impact upon the viewer. The psychological significance that is based on the viewer's previous experiences, color associations, cultural conditioning, societal influences, frame of mind, and personality all play into the final interpretation. It is truly a fascinating pathway to the ultimate perception of color.

15 What is the difference between iridescence, pearlescence, and opalescence, and why are we so attracted by the effects?

Pearlescence is an effect that resembles a lustrous surface that displays subtle pearl-like variations. Iridescence is marked by rainbow colors that appear to move and change as the viewing angle changes. Another meaning of iridescence, although less definitive, is having a lustrous or brilliant appearance or quality. Opalescence is defined as showing or possessing shimmering milky colors that are similar to those seen in opals and can be of almost any color. Many times these terms are used interchangeably, as it is as much about the undulating qualities and the effects they achieve as it is about color.

PHOTO: DON PAULSON

Social anthropologists tell us that people have always been attracted to these effects as the glistening movements remind us of bodies of water; and, as humans cannot live without water, we are constantly drawn to any surface that repeats its motions. It is an interesting concept and one that holds water. (I couldn't resist that!)

16 Can color memories and perceptions be passed on through our DNA?

Experts who have studied the subject believe that we are linked to the past in many ways through our DNA. They believe that deeply imbedded in the human psyche are connecting links to the distant past. Ancient memories, as they are called, live on through our biochemistry and through our senses and neural system, affecting our emotions, reflexes, and perceptions. What is often referred to as "intuition" may actually be a recollection of ancient memories that are passed on from generation to generation.

Each of us has approximately 100,000 generations of "successful" ancestors. They are successful because they survived! Think of how many "great-greats" you would have to repeat to go back that far. There is a continuing stream of DNA that connects us to all of our ancestors. The belief is that responses to color and patterns in ancient memory are most often on a subconscious level and imprinted in our psyches.

Human origins are believed to have come out of a semi-arid environment characterized by grasses and scattered trees, grading into open plains or woodlands, hosting a variety of foliage and long views that disclosed water and natural resources.

Most generations lived completely in the "natural world" without benefit of synthetic fibers and colors. Their "comfort level" came from using patterns and colors indigenous to their surrounding world.

Some researchers believe that a level of familiarity, connection, and reassurance will result from using a combination of patterning and color that utilizes primal, instinctive, natural themes. These are the visual triggers that bring a sense of being in harmony with humankind's earliest time on Earth.

Whether you agree or disagree, it is a fascinating concept and may very well explain why many people feel so intimately connected to using natural, simple, and organic themes and colors in their homes. Of course, as discussed in Chapter 6, Decorating Your Home, there are many reasons why people are drawn to certain colors and moods, but this adds another dimension to our thinking.

THE HUMAN EYE is inevitably drawn to lustrous surfaces. We are fascinated and intrigued by colors that appear to undulate, change, glimmer, radiate, or shimmer.

PHOTO: DON PAULSON

CHAPTER TWO

Your Personal Response to Color

Certain colors and color

combinations evoke

all sorts of reactions, both

positive and negative.

THE RESPONSE TO COLOR is a primitive one, more emotional than intellectual for most people. How people respond to color can give you some insight into their social orientation, their maturity (not always a good thing!), their cultural conditioning, self-esteem, and creativity. And it will also give you some clearer personal insights into all of the above.

1

How and why do we develop color preferences?

Some people can respond instantly to the question "What's your favorite or least favorite color?" Others have to ponder a bit. The best way to really determine your best liked or least liked color is to take the following quiz.

COLOR WORD ASSOCIATION QUIZ

THE COLOR WORD ASSOCIATION QUIZ provides you with an opportunity to inventory your reactions and associations to a wide variety of hues in every color family: light, medium, dark, or bright. This is a vital part of your personal discovery process brought on by your reaction to each color. Get into a quiet place with good daylight and try to avoid any distractions. You may have strong positive or negative reactions to some of the colors and feel indifferent to others. There are no right or wrong answers, only *your* answers. Don't agonize or analyze now (there will be time for that later!). Simply record the first word or words that pop into your mind.

Note: If you do not like the color shown as an example but generally like the color family, please treat this sample as the closest representative color. For example, if burgundy red is a color you generally like but the deep blue-red shown here is not the precise shade you like, use the color shown as a representative of that family.

After you take the quiz, choose one of these colors as your favorite and one as your least favorite color.

Immediately next to the column describing the color, there are three additional columns marked "P" (Positive), "N" (Negative), "I" (Indifferent). Check your P, N, or I reaction immediately after writing the descriptive word next to the color.

Spark Your Imagination
Listed below are words that frequently appear when people define their color associations. You may use these words, but feel free to use your own words, and they may give you even more personal insights.

Cover all the chips on these pages except the chip you are considering. You may change your attitude about certain colors as you continue to learn more about them or examine your feelings about them. But for now, it's important to record your immediate reaction to each color.

warm	cool	hot	cold	sterile
inviting	masculine	feminine	unisex	sea
earth	sky	ocean	happy	sad
tranquil	exciting	stimulating	dynamic	speedy
restful	fresh	refreshing	sexy	romantic
sunny	hard	soft	loud	subtle
neutral	classic	bland	ugly	beautiful
pretty	disgusting	fun	harsh	insipid
garish	fuzzy	sweet	sour	approachable
nurturing	friendly	juice	sensual	comforting
sensual	classy	peace	quiet	noisy
outgoing	sticky	grief	powerful	nauseating
powerful	basic	strong	passionate	weak
tasteful	elegant	expensive	regal	gregarious
cheap	tacky	rich	robust	dirty
clean	cleansing	serious	heavenly	mysterious
spiritual	serious	secure	rooted	nature
natural	artificial	smooth	tough	traditional

YOUR PERSONAL RESPONSE TO COLOR

23

1. Bright Yellow

Reaction:
❏ Positive   ❏ Negative   ❏ Indifferent

Associations: _____

_____

2. Light Yellow

Reaction:
❏ Positive   ❏ Negative   ❏ Indifferent

Associations: _____

_____

3. Golden Yellow

Reaction:
❏ Positive   ❏ Negative   ❏ Indifferent

Associations: _____

_____

4. Bright Chartreuse

Reaction:
❏ Positive   ❏ Negative   ❏ Indifferent

Associations: _____

_____

5. Bright Green

Reaction:
❏ Positive   ❏ Negative   ❏ Indifferent

Associations: _____

_____

6. Olive Green

Reaction:
❏ Positive   ❏ Negative   ❏ Indifferent

Associations: _____

_____

7. Dark Green

Reaction:
❏ Positive   ❏ Negative   ❏ Indifferent

Associations: _____

_____

8. Aqua

Reaction:
❏ Positive   ❏ Negative   ❏ Indifferent

Associations: _____

_____

9. Turquoise

Reaction:
❏ Positive   ❏ Negative   ❏ Indifferent

Associations: _____

_____

10. Teal

Reaction:
❏ Positive   ❏ Negative   ❏ Indifferent

Associations: _____

_____

11. Sky Blue

Reaction:
❏ Positive   ❏ Negative   ❏ Indifferent

Associations: _____

_____

12. Classic Blue

Reaction:
❏ Positive   ❏ Negative   ❏ Indifferent

Associations: _____

_____

13. NAVY BLUE

Reaction:
❏ Positive ❏ Negative ❏ Indifferent

Associations: _____

_____

14. BEIGE

Reaction:
❏ Positive ❏ Negative ❏ Indifferent

Associations: _____

_____

15. TERRA COTTA

Reaction:
❏ Positive ❏ Negative ❏ Indifferent

Associations: _____

_____

16. DARK BROWN

Reaction:
❏ Positive ❏ Negative ❏ Indifferent

Associations: _____

_____

17. CREAM

Reaction:
❏ Positive ❏ Negative ❏ Indifferent

Associations: _____

_____

18. PEACH

Reaction:
❏ Positive ❏ Negative ❏ Indifferent

Associations: _____

_____

19. ORANGE

Reaction:
❏ Positive ❏ Negative ❏ Indifferent

Associations: _____

_____

20. LIGHT PINK

Reaction:
❏ Positive ❏ Negative ❏ Indifferent

Associations: _____

_____

21. DUSTY PINK

Reaction:
❏ Positive ❏ Negative ❏ Indifferent

Associations: _____

_____

22. BRIGHT PINK

Reaction:
❏ Positive ❏ Negative ❏ Indifferent

Associations: _____

_____

23. FUCHSIA

Reaction:
❏ Positive ❏ Negative ❏ Indifferent

Associations: _____

_____

24. TRUE RED

Reaction:
❏ Positive ❏ Negative ❏ Indifferent

Associations: _____

_____

25. BRICK RED

Reaction:
❏ Positive ❏ Negative ❏ Indifferent

Associations: _____

_____

26. BURGUNDY

Reaction:
❏ Positive ❏ Negative ❏ Indifferent

Associations: _____

_____

27. LAVENDER ✓✓

Reaction:
❏ Positive ❏ Negative ❏ Indifferent

Associations: _____

_____

28. ORCHID ✓

Reaction:
❏ Positive ❏ Negative ❏ Indifferent

Associations: _____

_____

29. MAUVE

Reaction:
❏ Positive ❏ Negative ❏ Indifferent

Associations: _____

_____

30. VIOLET PURPLE ✓✓

Reaction:
❏ Positive ❏ Negative ❏ Indifferent

Associations: _____

_____

31. DEEP PURPLE ✓

Reaction:
❏ Positive ❏ Negative ❏ Indifferent

Associations: _____

_____

32. NEUTRAL GRAY ✓

Reaction:
❏ Positive ❏ Negative ❏ Indifferent

Associations: _____

_____

33. CHARCOAL GRAY ✓

Reaction:
❏ Positive ❏ Negative ❏ Indifferent

Associations: _____

_____

34. TAUPE ✓

Reaction:
❏ Positive ❏ Negative ❏ Indifferent

Associations: _____

_____

35. WHITE

Reaction:
❏ Positive ❏ Negative ❏ Indifferent

Associations: _____

_____

36. BLACK ✓

Reaction:
❏ Positive ❏ Negative ❏ Indifferent

Associations: _____

_____

Look back at your responses. Do you still feel that the color you chose as your favorite is actually your number one choice? How about your least favorite? Do you still agree? Your positive, negative, or indifferent responses will tell you even more. Obviously, you can't feel negative about a color you choose as a favorite nor positive about a color you dislike. "Indifferent" simply means you don't feel one way or another. Your word associations will give you some insights about your reactions to color and an opportunity for some interesting self-discovery.

Colors evoke emotions and associations to events long past, some pleasant and others very negative. Your reactions to colors can definitely be influenced by your personal experience. For example, one of my clients had a real aversion to lime green, key lime pie green, to be exact. When I asked him if he knew why he disliked the color so much, he told me it reminded him of the time when he was about six years old. His mom had baked several pies and left them on the stove to cool. When Mom took one of the pies to a neighbor next door, the six-year-old found the temptation too much to ignore and, with the help of the family dog, wolfed down an entire pie.

He paid his penance by promptly turning the color of the pie and whoops—the rest is history.

Some colorful memories in your own personal history you might recall, as my client did, but others are so deeply buried in your psyche that you forget the specific incident. But you never really forget the color. You can react subliminally to a color and not be consciously aware of the reason that you are so turned off by it.

Your judgment of color is not only based on what you *see*, but also on what you *feel*. Those feelings are extremely important. I could tell you until I was blue in the face that your best colors are in the yellow-green family because your eyes are yellow-green. But if your internal tape recorder goes on instant rewind to an unpleasant experience (like too much key lime pie!) your recorder will instantly eject my suggestion. I might be able to convince you otherwise, but your initial reaction would be negative.

PHOTO: DON PAULSON

REACTIONS TO COLORS—positive or negative—are often attached to childhood recollections. Spending summer weekends at the beach might be so etched in memory that warm sandy beige, a dazzling sun, clean, watery, cool blues and blue-greens will forever evoke happy memories, consistently inspiring that combination in clothing or, more often, decorating the home.

Conversely, if your grandmother's eyes were **Cornflower Blue** and they always sparkled with love and approval whenever she saw you, chances are more than likely that blue is going to be one of your favorite colors. If you inherited those beautiful blue eyes, the probability is even greater that blue is one of your favorite colors.

You can disregard a potentially wonderful color because of some experience long past that has no bearing on today. The emotional impact of color can be awesome or awful. Does the word "orchid" recall the first prom corsage you ever got (or gave) or does it remind you of your first post-prom hangover? Often you don't consciously recall the actual experience, but you never really forget anything you've ever learned; you just place it in that amazing storehouse called the brain.

Fortunately, many color-related childhood memories are positive, and studies tell us this continues into adulthood—most people have far more positive responses than negative. Every green-eyed person can relate to the compliments they got when as children they wore green. As adults, that approval continues and green remains their favorite color. We all need "warm fuzzies," so every time we wear a color that evokes a positive response, a bell rings in our psyches signaling approval.

Was **Ginger** the color (and the name) of your favorite plushy toy that accompanied you to bed every night when you were a little person? Or was it the color of the big overgrown scary gingerbread man who either chased you in a recurring nightmare or that you just knew was hiding under the bed waiting to gobble off your dangling foot?

Certain colors and color combinations will evoke all sorts of reactions, positive or negative, as you never really forget anything. You just deposit it in your memory bank for future withdrawals.

2 Is an eye for color like an ear for music? Are we born with a sense of color?

Although we may be predisposed to certain artistic abilities through our DNA, an eye for color can be acquired through the learning process. Some people are not born child prodigies excelling at piano, yet through instruction and practice, they learn to play well enough to satisfy their needs. They may never perform like a concert pianist or a world famous jazz musician, but they still manage to get a great deal of enjoyment and sense of satisfaction out of playing.

The same holds true for color. You may not have been born with artistic ability, but you can learn how to use color so that it will work wonders for you and give you tremendous satisfaction. When you arrange flowers in a vase, take a photograph, place food on a plate, or choose the right tie, you are the artist.

It's not just about taking Introductory Color 101, but it's also about observing and paying attention to detail. There are numerous books and magazines, catalogs, store displays, and web sites, as well as the standard color courses that are dedicated to style and color. These resources not only educate, but also they help to jump-start your imagination and sharpen your creative "eye."

3

Can color likes and dislikes tell us something about our personalities?

Absolutely. After reading various books or articles that I have written, people will often tell me how close color preferences can come to describing their personalities.

Do remember that your likes and dislikes can and do change over the years. Your responses simply tell you where you are at this particular time. Your preferences may also reveal some of your secret desires. For example, if you chose red as your favorite color, you may not see yourself as sexy or high energy, so you undoubtedly have some hidden desires that you have never acted on but would love to express. Maybe now is the time to become more like your favorite color!

Having a favorite color doesn't mean that you surround yourself with it or wear it constantly. It simply means that something special happens every time you look at that color.

For your amazement or amusement, the following is a compilation of what your favorite or least favorite colors say about you.

4

Red is my favorite (or least favorite) color. What does that say about me?

PHOTO: CHICO'S RETAIL SERVICES, INC.

FAVORITE: Just as red sits on top of the rainbow, you like to stay on top of things. You have a zest for life. Remember that red can speed up the pulse, increase the respiration rate, and raise blood pressure. It is associated with fire, heat, and blood, so it is impossible to ignore. And so are you (or would like to be).

The key words associated with red are winner, achiever, intense, impulsive, active, competitive, daring, aggressive, and passionate. Red people are exciting, animated, optimistic, emotional, and extroverted. Desire is the key word. They hunger for the fullness of experience and living. Nothing is ever done "halfway."

Since you crave so much excitement in your life, routine can drive you to distraction. Restlessness can make you fickle in your pursuit of new things to turn you on. You have to temper that energy so that you don't exhaust yourself and everyone around you. It is hard for you to be objective, and you can be opinionated. You have a tendency to listen to what others tell you and then do whatever you please. Patience is not one of your virtues.

THE CHOICE OF come-hither red as a favorite color reveals a great deal about a person's personality. Red's bright intensity doesn't meekly ask for a glance, it commands attention, and that is precisely why lovers of this high voltage hue love to wear it.

However, you are an exciting person to be with, always stimulating, impetuous, and up for adventure. The world would be a dull place without red people.

LEAST FAVORITE: Since red is primarily associated with a zest for life, excitement, and passion, a dislike of this hue could mean that these feelings are a bit much for you to handle at this point in your life. Perhaps you are bothered by the aggressiveness and intensity that red signifies. Or perhaps you would really like more fulfillment but are afraid to get involved. People who are irritable, ill, exhausted, or bothered by many problems often reject red and turn to the calmer colors for rest and relaxation. They are very self-protective.

5 Pink is my favorite (or least favorite) color. What does that say about me?

FAVORITE: If your favorite pink is vivid and bright, then you need to look at the traits listed under red. Hot pink is definitely more akin to the mother color with a matching personality.

But if your preferences lean to softer pinks, these are a softened red that tempers passion with purity. It is associated with romance, sweetness, delicacy, refinement, and tenderness. People who prefer soft pinks are interested in the world around them, but they do not throw themselves into participating with the ardor of the red person. As a result, pinks have energy, but not the kind that drains everyone around them. Violence in any form is upsetting to them.

At one time pink was considered exclusively feminine, like the frosting on a little girl's birthday cake. However, now that it is no longer considered "less macho" for men to exhibit sensitive, so-called "feminine traits," many men are more comfortable with pink.

If you love pink, you are talented and have subdued drive, charm, and warmth, and are probably an incurable, candles-on-the-table kind of romantic. Pink people are refined and friendly but tend to keep inner feelings hidden from the people they don't know intimately.

LEAST FAVORITE: Soft, medium tints do not evoke much emotion—some people are indifferent to pink. It is sweetness, innocence, and naiveté—red with the passion removed. So, if you dislike pink, you are looking for excitement in your life, and pink simply will not do it for you. You are probably ambitious (and fairly obvious about it), so that pink simply isn't red enough for you, but a hot pink would work.

6 Yellow is my favorite (or least favorite) color. What does that say about me?

FAVORITE: Yellow is luminous and warm because it is strongly associated with sunshine. It sparkles with optimistic activity. Yellow people are highly original, imaginative, idealistic, creative, artistic, and seek "enlightenment." As a result, they love novelty and challenge, and have inquiring minds. Although they may or may not be intellectual, they love playing "mind games."

You are a playful friend and companion. Your ambitions are often realized, and you usually have a sunny disposition. Because yellow people are optimists, they are great people to confide in as their cheerfulness, the "cup is half full" kind of reaction to most issues, leads to words of encouragement and positive reinforcement.

PHOTO: DON PAULSON

A glorious summer sunset best reflects the personality of people who love both yellow and orange. Their sunny dispositions radiate with imagination and creativity, and they are on a constant quest for enlightenment. The orange aspect of their personalities makes them even more adventurous and enthusiastic.

As a co-worker, this is not the kind of person with a "been there, done that" attitude. New ideas and concepts stimulate them.

They can be egotistical, however, and do not like to be second best. You can be generous, yet impatient with other people's ideas if they seem less well thought out than yours. You are genuinely concerned about the good of society, but generally spend more time talking about it than actually doing anything about it! Yellow people are perfectionists, but can also be joyful about it.

LEAST FAVORITE: If you dislike yellow, you usually dislike the qualities that this luminous color has. You are a realist—a practical, down-to-earth person, and probably critical of others who are not. You are skeptical of new ideas and rather than try something innovative, you prefer to concentrate on things you know you can accomplish. Guaranteed results are important to you because you like to protect yourself from disappointment.

7 Orange is my favorite (or least favorite) color. What does that say about me?

FAVORITE: Orange is a combination of red and yellow, so it takes on many of the characteristics of both colors. It is vibrant and warm, open to challenge and activity. Orange has the physical force of red, but it is less intense, less passionate. Lovers of this color work and play hard, and are adventurous and enthusiastic with a great sense of humor.

You are good-natured, expansive, and extroverted, with a disposition as bright as your favorite color, and you like to be with people. Your ideas are unique and you have strong determination. You are more agreeable than aggressive, the perfect salesperson. Success in business can come easily to this gregarious, charming, often charismatic person. At work and at home, they are motivators.

However, orange people can be fickle as they are people-collectors. It has been said that your latest friend is your best friend. Orange lovers make for undependable mates—they're always looking for new worlds to conquer!

If your preferences tend to the peach tones, you have all of the same traits as the orange person, but you are much less assertive about it. You work hard, but your play (especially sports) activities are more as an observer than a participant. You're friendly and charming as well, but in a much more subtle way!

LEAST FAVORITE: Life is definitely not a dish of gumdrops for the rejecter of orange. Nothing flamboyant appeals to you. You dislike too much partying, hilarity, loud laughter, showing off, and obvious intimacy. As a result, you may be difficult to get to know, if not a loner. You prefer a few genuine close friends to a large circle of acquaintances, and once you make friends, they're your friends forever.

8 Brown is my favorite (or least favorite) color. What does that say about me?

FAVORITE: The color of the Earth is the hue that is associated with substance and stability. A preference for brown means you have a steady, reliable character with a keen sense of duty and responsibility. You are the down-to-earth person with a subtle sense of humor. Browns love simplicity, comfort, quality, harmony, hearth, and home. Above all, they are grounded. But it's not all about homespun Mother Earth themes—remember that polished leathers, deep mahoganies, and a warm espresso can also speak of the same characteristics described above, with a richer sophistication.

You are a loyal friend, understanding but firm. Brown people have strong views and may be intolerant of others who think, talk, or act too quickly. You strive to be good money managers (we won't say "cheap") and drive a good bargain.

You are the person who might find it difficult to be carefree and spontaneous, but will often rebel internally against accepting things the way they are. You feel very uncomfortable about losing control, but will work hard to change a situation that seems unjust or unfair.

You'd make a good marriage partner and a good parent because you have a strong need for security and a sense of belonging. Family life is very important to you.

LEAST FAVORITE: You probably fantasize about a lot of things, perhaps traveling with a circus or racing cars. Novelty excites you and routine drives you crazy. You are witty, impetuous, and generous. Living on a farm is not for you. Homespun people bore you. You do like people, but they must be bright and outgoing. A meaningful relationship with you could be risky business—it's hard to get you to sit still!

9 Beige is my favorite (or least favorite) color. What does that say about me?

FAVORITE: Beige people have many of the same characteristics as brown, though they are probably less intense. Creamy beiges and honeyed tones take on a lot of yellow qualities, while rose-beiges take on pink characteristics. You are warm, appreciate quality, and are carefully neutral in most situations. You are usually well adjusted and practical, not prone to flights of fancy. Although this may sound as if you are rather lackluster or uninteresting, the world needs steadfast, reasonable people who, at the same time, possess a willing warmth.

As beige is a color associated with elements of the eternal—desert sand, pyramids, and the Sphinx—it is a quiet strength that describes your character. You are a good and fair counselor, willing and able to look at both sides of a picture.

LEAST FAVORITE: You are less frenetic and impetuous than a disliker of brown, but have many of the same characteristics. Beige represents to you a beige existence—boring and tiresome. You hate routine and practicality, preferring fantasy to reality.

10 Green is my favorite (or least favorite) color. What does that say about me?

FAVORITE: Nature's most plentiful color promises a balance between warmth and coolness, so green people are usually stable and balanced types. This is the good citizen, concerned parent, involved neighbor, and PTA member—the joiner of clubs, organizations, especially those that are charitable. You are fastidious, kind, and generous, possessing some of the same traits as blue people, but just as green is a bit warmer than blue, people who prefer green are a bit warmer and approachable.

It is important for you to win the admiration of peers so you are often a "do-gooder." In an organization, you are the soldier who takes on responsibility and gets the job done. You are a caring companion, loyal friend, partner or lover, with a high moral sense, and are super sensitive to doing the right thing. Your expectation is that everyone around you (including your children, spouses, or significant others) will be the same way and do the right thing.

You are intelligent and understand new concepts. You are less inclined, however, to risk something new than to do what is popular, conventional, and sensible. The bad news about green people is that they often have big appetites for food. If you are dieting, it is difficult for you to lose your lumps. The worst vice for a green is the tendency to gossip. Are you a little green with envy?

LEAST FAVORITE: Since lovers of green are usually very social joiners and strive to be involved in causes, dislikers of green will often put those qualities down. You may have an unfulfilled need to be recognized that causes you to pull away from people rather than join them. You don't like thinking, looking, and doing things the way you see the majority of people thinking, looking, and doing them. Company picnics or chatty cocktail parties are not your thing.

Biliousness and certain body functions are often associated with yellow-green, as are snakes, lizards, dragons, and various other creepy crawlies. Did something slithery frighten you as a child?

11

Blue is my favorite (or least favorite) color. What does that say about me?

FAVORITE: The color of tranquility and peace, blue tends to be the most preferred color universally. Although cool and confident (or wishing to be), blues can be vulnerable. You are trusting and need to be trusted. You are sensitive to the needs of others and form strong attachments, and are deeply hurt if your trust has been betrayed.

You are somewhat social but prefer sticking to your own close circle of friends. You think twice before speaking or acting out. You are generally conservative, even-tempered, and reliable, all excellent traits in a parent, employee, co-worker, or spouse. If vibrant blues are more to your liking, then you need to have a bit more excitement in your life and tend to be more gregarious.

Because of the highly developed sense of responsibility of the blue personality, you must be careful of perfectionist tendencies that may make you unrealistically demanding. Your gentleness, however, will usually win out.

LEAST FAVORITE: A dislike of blue may mean restlessness—a need to break away from the sameness that bores you. Perhaps you would like to change your job, or even your life, and long for more excitement. You might be tired of being "depended on," but your conscience

LOVERS OF BLUE constantly search for the quiet, Zen-like perfection of peaceful calm. For the true blue lovers, there is ultimate satisfaction in the serenity that only blue can offer.

PHOTO: © DYNASTY LANE

THE COLOR ANSWER BOOK

34

makes you stay. You wish that you were wealthy or brilliant (or both) because that would enable you to have all the good things in life without working so hard. Deeper blues may mean sadness and melancholy to you—blue may simply give you the blues.

12 Blue-green is my favorite (or least favorite) color. What does that say about me?

FAVORITE: Since this is a marriage of both blue and green, many of the traits will be combined. But there are added dimensions. You are sensitive, but also cool, self-assured, and (usually) stable.

You help others and usually manage your own affairs very well, you are a good communicator. Courtesy and charm are characteristics, too. Clear turquoise and aquas are soothers and calmers and, at the same time, invigorating, and this is a good description of you.

Social interaction comes easily to you. You are neat and well groomed, but narcissism can also play a part in this personality. Blue-greens and green-blues love to dress up to get the admiration of others, but along with admiration you may also provoke some of the "blue-green-eyed monsters."

LEAST FAVORITE: Since love of blue-green means orderliness and neatness, dislike of blue-green means that, as messy as you'd like to be, a little voice inside you (was it your mother or your father?) keeps telling you to clean up your room. As much as you try to ignore it, it won't go away. You really love to relax more and not pay attention to petty details. You prefer earthy types to fussy people.

13 Purple is my favorite (or least favorite) color. What does that say about me?

FAVORITE: This hue has an aura of mystery and intrigue. When it leans to the red side it embraces more sensuality, just as red does. When it is closer to blue there is a greater understanding of the quieting aspect of spiritualism. So a description of the purple person has a great deal to do with their preferences for red-purple or blue-purple. As a result, the purple person is intuitive, imaginative, and highly creative, with a quick perception of supernatural ideas.

Artists, or others who like to consider themselves unconventional or different from the common herd, often prefer purple. Purple people have a greater sense of the intangible. They don't have to see it to believe it.

You are often generous and, at times, charming. Purple is also associated with wit, keen observation, super sensitivity, vanity, and moodiness. Because purple is a combination of red and blue, which are opposites in many ways, you often have conflicting traits. You are constantly trying to balance those opposites—the excitement of red with the tranquility of blue.

It has been said that purple people are easy to live with but hard to know. You can be secretive and enigmatic so that even when you seem to confide freely, your closest friends never completely understand you. But when they want truly imaginative ideas and inspiration, they will come to you.

LEAST FAVORITE: If you are anti-purple, you need sincerity, honesty, and a lack of pretense in your life. You do not like to get involved unless you know exactly what you are getting yourself into. You usually exercise good judgment. Frankness is a quality you look for in your friends. You may not have a particular artistic talent, but you would make a good critic.

Because of purple's association with royalty, purple may seem puffed up and pompous to you or, because of its association with mourning, you may see it as melancholy. In certain areas of the world, bright purple is worn by ladies of questionable reputation. Perhaps you are still hearing that little voice in your ear telling you that nice people don't wear purple. If so, it's time to get off the old track and on to a new way of thinking. Some of the most interesting and creative people use purple.

14 Lavender is my favorite (or least favorite) color. What does that say about me?

FAVORITE: People who love this tint use it sometimes to the exclusion of all other colors. Just as with purple, this person likes to be considered different. You are quick-witted, though not necessarily intellectual.

The lavender person seeks refinement in life. Yours is a fantasyland where ugliness and the baser aspects of life are ignored. Outward appearances are very important. Gentility and sentimental leanings also go along with this color, as do romance, nostalgia, and delicacy. Since lavender is first cousin to purple, you may aspire to creativity, but, if not capable of it, you tend to encourage those who do have talent.

Lavender has a rather ethereal quality, a gentle nature. And, just as in the healing qualities of the lavender flower, if this quiet hue is your preference, you are a seeker of peace, harmony, and well-being.

LEAST FAVORITE: Yours is a no-nonsense approach to life. You don't like others to be coy with you—you would rather they be direct. Nostalgia is not your thing; you live in the present. Just as with the anti-purple people, you don't like superficiality in manners or appearance, and you usually let people know about it (or wish that you had). You may also see lavender as insipid or aging.

15 Gray is my favorite (or least favorite) color. What does that say about me?

FAVORITE: People who prefer this most neutral of all shades are carefully neutral about life. You like to protect yourself from the hectic world, wrapping yourself with the security blanket of a noncommittal color. You prefer a secure, safe, balanced existence, and so unlike the reds in life, you never crave real excitement, just contentment.

It is important for you to maintain the status quo. Corporate life and working in a cubicle are not all that unappealing as you are inclined to be very focused and not easily distracted. If you prefer gray, you would be excellent within a corporate structure, very supportive and even-keeled.

You have often made compromises in your lifestyles. You are practical and calm, and do not like to attract attention. You are willing to work hard (the gray flannel suit) and to be of service. You are the middle-of-the-road type, cool, conservative, composed, rock-solid, and reliable. These are not very flashy traits, but very fundamental in both relationships and many businesses.

LEAST FAVORITE: To dislike gray is to dislike neutrality. You would rather be right or wrong, but never indifferent. Routine bores you. You look for a richer, fuller life. This may lead you to get into one involvement, hobby, or interest after another in the pursuit of happiness. Gray may also mean the subliminal reminder of eerie ghosts, ashes, cobwebs, and the dust of a haunted house, or other scary gray things.

16 Taupe is my favorite (or least favorite) color. What does that say about me?

FAVORITE: This color also speaks of neutrality, but combines the character and dependability of gray with the warmth of beige. You like classic looks and are careful about allowing too much excitement into your life. "Authentic" is a key word for you. You're practical, fair, well balanced, but not without warmth, and would make a good arbitrator.

LEAST FAVORITE: If taupe doesn't appeal to you, it may be because it is so balanced and classic. You'd rather make a more definite statement, whether with color or otherwise. You're probably not known for your subtlety.

17 Black is my favorite (or least favorite) color. What does that say about me?

Classic chic – good taste

FAVORITE: This is rarely chosen as a favorite color because it is actually the negation of color. The person who chooses black may have a number of conflicting attitudes. You may be conventional, conservative, and serious, or you may like to think of yourself as rather worldly or sophisticated. There is no question that black is the ultimate of classic chic and good taste, and that is how you like to see yourself and want others to view you.

You may also want to have an air of mystery, or, as in the language of the proverbial black negligée, seem very sexy. Wit, cleverness, personal security, and prestige are very important to you.

Above all, black is empowering as well as powerful, bringing with it a large level of confidence. You will never call a lot of attention to yourself, especially if everyone else is wearing black. It is definitely a big-city color as it provides a protective, well-accepted armor that will allow you to figuratively "fit in," and that is very important to you.

LEAST FAVORITE: Since black is the negation of color, it may be a total negative to you. It is the eternal mystery, the bottomless pit, the black hole, the Halloween witch and her black cat. It may represent death and mourning to you. Things that go bump in the night are black. Were you frightened by the dark in your childhood? That experience could be buried in the darkest recesses of your mind and may still haunt you when you look at anything black. Black may simply be too heavy or depressing for you to handle at this point in your life.

You are uncomfortable with the super-sophisticated and feel insecure in their company. You like "real" people and are not dazzled by dignitaries.

18

White is my favorite (or least favorite) color. What does that say about me?

FAVORITE: White is cleanliness and purity, and those who prefer white are neat and immaculate in their clothing and homes. You are inclined to not only be self sufficient, but also be a cautious buyer and shrewd trader, a bit critical and fussy. If you got a spot on your tie or scarf in a restaurant, you would summon a glass of water immediately to clean it off.

This is a person who is so neat and tidy that everything has its place. Organization is a priority, and messiness is not easily tolerated. Most of us could use a friend or employee like this to help us dig out from under (as long as they don't drive us crazy in their quest for neatness). Their credo is "A place for everything and everything in its place!"

White also signifies innocence. It is a recall of youth and simplicity, and a longing to be young again. People who prefer white would prefer stepping back to a more innocent time.

LEAST FAVORITE: Since white represents cleanliness and purity, to dislike white does not exactly mean that you are a messy and totally disorganized person, but it does mean that you have never been obsessed with order. You are not very fussy. Things that are a little off-center are much more interesting to you than those that are perfectly in line. A little dust on the shelves or on yourself doesn't throw you into a spasm of cleaning. You are not very uptight and are easy to be with. You may see white as sterile and connect it with a hospital stay or visits to the dentist.

19

What does it mean if you have more than one favorite color or if you prefer colors that are mixtures?

The late Faber Birren, author of many color books and the inventor, so to speak, of utilizing a psychological approach in the color-consulting industry, felt that people who preferred basic or primary colors had fairly "open" characters with strong and well-directed interests. To prefer more complex colors such as blue-green over blue or green indicates, not surprisingly, a more complex personality.

Another example of a more complex color is **Aragon**, a combination of orange and brown. If this would be a favorite color, then you might have some of the traits of both of those hues. The problem is that some of the underlying colors may be in conflict with each other. Brown is emphasis on family life, whereas orange is fickle. How much of you is orange and how much is brown? That's an interesting question that only you can answer.

Purple is another example of a complex color. It is not often chosen as a favorite color as many people are rather befuddled by it—they just don't "get" purple. It truly takes a practiced or creative eye to appreciate purple as it is a combination of seemingly contradictory traits. Red is excitement and energy, while blue is more often placid and serene. When these two colors are combined and purple is created, there is this push-pull effect that presents a real challenge. And the challenge to make it work well is what makes purple so exciting to creative, artistic types. It is the complexity of the color that is so appealing to them.

If you like lots of different colors, then you are also a creative type, one most likely to work professionally with color. For you, it would be like having to choose a favorite child! Some "experts" have proclaimed that people who choose many colors have fragmented personalities. I simply don't buy that theory. My own experience has been that people who have a willingness to work with many colors and love a variety of colors are more open. They allow the child within them to come to the surface and are far less rigid than those with very dogmatic likes and dislikes.

In analyzing why people choose what they choose, we have to be careful not to over-generalize. Many times people select a dark shade out of necessity either because they work in a big dirty city and it doesn't show dirt, or because dark shades are slenderizing, or they choose neutrals because they "go with everything." But there is always a message implied and in the examples above, the message is "I'm practical!"

20 Can choosing "new" colors help to change your life?

I don't think that it can necessarily change your life, as it takes a lot more than color to do that, but it can certainly readjust your attitude and outlook. We have all seen the magical differences that color can make, as in the amazing cosmetic "makeovers." A new shade of lipstick, a little blush, a flattering new hair color, or a fun trend color in a shirt can help to make you feel better when you need some instant gratification.

We have all experienced the uplifting effect of newly painted walls over a dismally somber color. The change isn't as instant as in clothing and it's a lot more work, but no less gratifying. Many people who have reinvented or remade their lives, such as divorcing a spouse or moving to a new area, choose new colors to go with their new personas or their new spaces. It certainly can help to provide a fresh new perspective.

It is often not the specific color, but the lightness, brightness, or depth of a shade that can make a difference. If you are finding that you gravitate to lighter colors, this often represents a longing to escape from the harsher realities of life. For many cultures, darkness means depression and brightness signifies happiness. Again, overgeneralization is dangerous and should not suggest that every time you wear something dark you are feeling depressed. But if you wear dark shades habitually to the exclusion of all other colors, there might be a deeper reason that you should examine. A heavy mood may make you unconsciously choose dark colors.

Try some self-help therapy with an injection of color. The next time you are feeling sad or depressed, if you are wearing dark or neutral shades, switch to brighter colors. Even if it is just a scarf or a tie, you might be surprised at what it does to elevate your mood. It is possible that it could be a self-fulfilling prophesy, as cheerful colors often make other people react to you in a friendly way and that, in turn, helps to elevate your mood.

Bright colors certainly are equated with outgoing, optimistic, and creative personalities. This is true to a large extent, but you don't want to turn on the brights all the time as there is also the perception that people who consistently wear vivid colors have a real need to attract attention. As in every area of life, the key word is balance. Which brings us to the next question and answer.

21 What is meant by the term "afterimage" and how does it work?

Interestingly, these amazing bodies that we inhabit contain a mechanism that always provides an instant visual balance. If you studied color in school, you probably had a teacher who introduced you to this fascinating and fun experiment. Study any color surface for a few seconds, look away at another plain surface, preferably white, and you will see the afterimage or the simultaneous contrast to the color you were studying. It is actually the complementary or opposite color on the color wheel. If you were concentrating on red, you will see a bluish-green, if it was yellow, you will see its opposite in purple (violet), and if it was blue, you will see the complement in an orange tone.

Note that every color registers an opposite in "temperature," a warm opposite a cool. This phenomenon is a graphic example of the body's instantaneous ability to restore balance. It is called homeostasis, literally meaning "a state of equilibrium." Each of us has an innate need to maintain both an internal and external equilibrium. We seek it physically, spiritually, emotionally, and aesthetically, and we are constantly playing a balancing act to maintain that equilibrium. Color can help us in that quest, especially in our homes.

Although we may not be overtly aware of it (but you will be from now on), our innate longing for balance makes us search for the balanced use of color. If we have used too many hot or warm colors in a room, our eyes search for something cool to rest on. Often, it's a green plant or a window that reveals some greenery. The opposite is true as well. If we are in a cold, sterile blue-white environment, we look for something in a warm color to turn up the heat a bit. For example, **Glacier** blue and **Frost** green might be wonderfully refreshing, cooling shades, but a dollop of **Banana Cream** will keep the temperature from turning too icy cold.

In decorating our environments, whether in a home or office, we feel most comfortable and balanced in an atmosphere that sets a dominant temperature and then provides the presence of the opposite temperature. To get a real sense of warmth or coolness, one color temperature must dominate. Dividing the atmosphere into half warm and half cool won't work—one temperature must be prevalent, so that 75 or 85 percent of the color scheme is either warm or cool. If you live in a cool climate, you might welcome warmer colors as the dominant theme or vice versa. It all depends on your comfort level and personal reaction to color.

When in doubt, always choose a favorite as the dominant color story because, in the long run, it will simply please you more, and that is exactly what color is all about—providing a pleasant, enjoyable comfort level.

THERE IS NO DOUBT that the red carpet is center stage in this room. There are additional warm tones in a yellow lamp, beige chairs and light wood tones. To keep the atmosphere from getting too hot (especially in a warm climate), there is the necessary balance of cooling textures such as metal, glass, and the ultimate cool touch of green foliage.

PHOTO: MASLAND CARPETS

PHOTO: GILD THE LILY

CHAPTER THREE

Color On You

As opposed to the extended

world around you, clothing

is your "second skin,"

a vital clue to your persona.

ATTRACTIVE AND FLATTERING color in clothing, cosmetics, and hair is a huge confidence booster. Who among us hasn't stood a little taller when we bask in the glow of "That red dress is fabulous on you," "What a great green tie … it makes your eyes look fantastic," "Have you done something new to your hair … it looks great," "Turquoise is your color;" and when you are wearing a dark "power" color, the ultimate, "You look so slim, have you lost weight?" Color has a major impact on the way we see ourselves as well as on the way others view us.

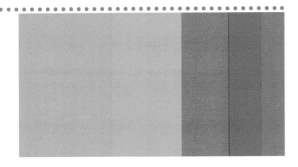

CLOTHING CAN BE a beautiful expression of wearable art, a moving collage of colors that, above every other consideration, makes you feel wonderful. And, if it is a special occasion, you need to feel special.

In this diaphanous dress, the striking use of **Geranium Pink**, **Burnt Coral** and **Tea Rose** is offset by contrasting subtle shadings of **Nile Blue** and **Wild Dove**.

Colors, left to right: **Geranium Pink, Burnt Coral, Tea Rose, Nile Blue, Wild Dove**

Color is so important in our perception of others that the first thing we see when someone approaches us from a distance is the color of his or her clothing. Are they a member of the tribe, friend or foe, a policeman coming to protect us? The closer a person approaches, the more space he or she occupies in our visual field and the greater its effect on our nervous system. There are other clues, of course, such as verbal cues, body language, scents, and intuition; but the color of the clothing, as well as other body enhancement colors, has the most immediate effect.

As opposed to the extended world around you, clothing is your "second skin," a vital clue to your persona. Clothes create your intimate environment. You choose clothing (and cosmetic/hair) colors the same way that you choose anything else in your environment—because they create a pleasing and comfortable atmosphere, you have an affinity to those colors and, most importantly, they raise your confidence level.

1 What colors make you appear thinner?

Everyone knows that black makes the wearer appear slimmer. But do you really want to wear black all the time? Bor-ing! There is no question but that darker colors make an area shrink, so think about shades other than black for some variety. In addition to the obvious **Charcoal Gray** and **True Navy**, there are colors like **Deep Claret**, **Earth Red**, **Ruby Wine**, **Plum Purple**, **Skipper Blue**, **Mallard Blue** (a deep blue green), **Dark Ivy**, **Chocolate Brown**, and **Cappuccino** that are slenderizing, although some of the names may be fattening! Midtone shades, such as **Dusty Rose**, **Toasted Almond**, **Cadet** blue, **Fawn**, and **Deep Taupe** are "thinning" as well.

2 What colors make you appear younger?

There are no absolute guarantees here, but the colors that look most like a healthy baby's skin are always youthful. If you are Caucasian or Asian, it would be the shades most similar to the blush tones of **Rosewater**, **Seashell Pink**, or **Peach Fuzz**. Those colors are equally flattering to dark skins, with the addition of **Mocha Bisque** and **Toffee**.

3 What colors make you appear richer?

In the "olden days" wealthy people often wore very understated, subtle tones as they were considered "high class." Bright colors were for the golf course or resort wear. That is no longer true as more upscale designers revisited the color wheel and brought more so-called ethnic influence into their designs, and these colors are often vibrant and exciting. The best advice is to be certain that your clothing looks expensive, no matter what the price. For example, be certain the stitching matches the background fabric (unless it is contrasting topstitching) and that the plaids and checks match at the seams. Expensive-looking clothing has more to do with construction, workmanship, and quality fabric than about color these days.

4 According to the seasonal color theory, I was told that I was a "summer" when I was in my twenties, but now I feel like I need the bolder colors of winter. Can we change seasons with age?

Yes, you can certainly change "seasons" as a result of complexion, hair, and eye color changes. Yes, your eyes change color as well! Most everything fades and/or yellows with age. But before you get unduly depressed, the changes can be fun as they open up a whole new color vista. If your eyes are brown, for example, you will start to see interesting little flecks of green or gold and you might find yourself looking smashing in **Sage Green**, a color you have always loved but never thought you could wear.

Hair color changes can cause the most dramatic differences, at any age. If your brown hair turns gray (silver sounds much better), you might find that vibrant jewel tones really look wonderful on you. Conversely, a glowing "autumn" redhead who lightens into a warm honey blonde will find that a "summer" **Apricot** is less overpowering than an "autumn" **Carrot** orange.

If you still love the colors in your season, but find them less flattering as a result of the changes in your coloring, combine them in a print or pattern with some of your "new" colors. Then you will have the best of both color worlds. For example, the former redhead mentioned above might still love orange and apricot, and her brown eyes might still be flattered by a touch of those shades. Why not combine a tad of coral and a bit more apricot with a vibrant blue green (Mother Nature does it all the time!—just look at the garden). The jewel-tone green will contrast beautifully with the silver hair, and the warm tones will enhance the brown eyes.

5 Why do people wear so much black? Is it just easy, a statement about yourself, or that it makes you look thinner?

The answer is all of the above! First, as we all know, black is so practical and takes little planning to pull the pieces together. So it works well for travel, for work, and for evening wear, and accessorizing is never a problem as there are always black bags, coats, suits, and separates available. Black is definitely a statement as it is the ultimate power color, endowing the wearer with an elegant, classic look. You can spend very little or spend a lot on an outfit, and black rarely looks cheap (depending on the quality of the fabric). If your budget is limited (or not), black is the reliable, no-brainer as far as coordinating with other colors.

PHOTO: CHICO'S RETAIL SERVICES, INC.

IN ANY WARDROBE, there is truly no replacement for black. It is the color that spans all seasons. It is ageless since it never goes out of style; and it is not gender-specific since it is equally chic on both men and women.

People in large cities often wear black as they feel the need to be protected and to feel empowered. Black makes them feel less vulnerable. And when everyone else is wearing the same color, the message becomes: "I am part of the group."

If you are a real perfectionist the biggest problem is putting black pieces together that may be of slightly different undertones. A suit jacket, for example, that may be a brownish black and is worn with a pair of pants with a blue undertone can look tacky, so try to keep the undertones consistent. The *pièce de resistance* is that it does make the wearer look slimmer. When writers call to ask me, "What is the new black this season?" I answer by saying, "Black is the new black!" It is irreplaceable.

6 I was always told that gold and silver should never be worn together. Is that still true?

No, it is not, as evidenced by that very combination in some of the most beautiful, expensive pieces of jewelry that have been shown recently and will continue to be seen in the future. However, there is a rule of thumb that does enable us to combine metallic surfaces. It is all a matter of proportion.

As silver is cool and gold is warm, there is a rule of dominance that prevails when combining different color temperatures (warm and cool). The piece could be approximately 75 percent warm, or 75 percent cool, with the opposite temperature making up about 25 percent. This could vary somewhat, perhaps at 80 percent to 20 percent or 85 percent to 15 percent, but the point is that one temperature should be dominant, and the other subordinate. Asymmetry in design and color is more interesting than half warm and half cool, so it is best not to use 50 percent gold and 50 percent silver equally divided in one piece of jewelry.

Combining gold and silver also offers more versatility and opportunities in accessorizing. For example, a combination silver and gold bangle bracelet could be worn with either silver or gold bangles and/or necklace.

PHOTO: ROSS-SIMONS

A combination of both silver and gold makes for an excellent and versatile investment in jewelry. It extends the usage of the pieces to accessorize both warm and cool colors.

7 What colors will make me look sexy?

Sexy is a relative term. What one person finds appealing, another may not. However, the color that shows up most frequently on color word association tests as the sexiest shade is a vibrant **Lipstick Red**. It's a sexual signal that many animals and birds use to attract the opposite sex and, interestingly, humans do as well. They flush and blush, turning red with embarrassment or sexual energy. They use cosmetic enhancements like reddish lips, nails (fingers and toes), and cheeks.

It is the color that most represents sensuality in many cultures as it is often used symbolically to broadcast availability or preparation for marriage and mating rites. The use of red as a sexual signal by primitive tribes for body painting and dyes ultimately translated to a more sophisticated use of sensuous red in modern day makeup and clothing.

PHOTO: COMSTOCK.COM

THERE IS NO QUESTION that red is nature's sexual signal. Walk into a room in a red dress or a red sweater and all eyes will be on you in a nanosecond.

8 Are there any rules for appropriate shoe and stocking colors for women?

I prefer not using the word "rule" as styles can change. However, there are some fundamental when-in-doubt guidelines for both shoes and pantyhose.

Shoes

When wearing a light to medium value or neutral color, neutral-colored shoes work best. They may be somewhat lighter, darker, or the same color as the hemline. For example, a **Coral** dress with a **Cream Tan** shoe, or a skirt with a **Lavender**-colored background worn with a **Silver Gray** shoe. A classic taupe such as **Simply Taupe**, which is neither too beige nor too gray, is the most versatile of all of the neutrals.

Very dark hues in an outfit look best with dark shoes: shades such as **Jet Black**, **True Navy**, **Deep Taupe**, **Eggplant**, and **Deep Teal**. In fashion parlance, this is called stability—balancing of the darker shades on the upper body with those on the lower body. This is especially important for anyone whose proportions are wider below than above (almost everyone, unless you are a 5 foot 13 inch fashion model!)

Shoes can match the color of the outfit itself. This can be very dramatic or a "fun" look, as in **True Red** sandals to match a pair of shorts. A long **Emerald** green dress might be striking with matching shoes, but stripy black high-heeled sandals would work too, and be far more practical. Remember that wearing bright, light, white, or shiny textures in shoes will highlight your feet and legs. If you are self-conscious about the size of your feet or legs, you will be creating a focal point where you might least want it to be. For that reason, you can take more liberties with color when you are wearing full-length pants, as size is less of an issue because a long vertical line is presented.

Shoes (or boots) might also match something in the upper part of the outfit, such as a belt. This creates a connecting link that helps to tie everything together visually.

Stockings

A rule of thumb is to blend your stockings with your shoes. It will make you look "leggier" and especially sexy when the shoe and stocking both match the color of the skin. Light stockings go in and out of style, but just as with shoes, they need to link to something at the top of the body, such as a blouse.

Contrary to "conventional wisdom," dark stockings or pantyhose do not always make your legs look slimmer and light stockings do not always make your legs look heavier. It depends on how the look is put together. **True Navy** stockings under a **Light Gray** skirt will draw the eye directly to the point where the two colors come together and enlarge the legs by creating a horizontal line, but wearing light **Sand** stockings under a **Sand** skirt creates a longer line, especially when coordinated with **Sand**-colored shoes.

Trends may change, but these are the basic stocking/tights color families for women:

TAUPE: This is a gray-beige shade that blends so well with so many clothing colors. It's best with taupe, of course, but a good when-in-doubt shade.

BEIGE TO MEDIUM BROWN: Best with bone, off-white, and browns. These colors will function as neutrals if they blend with your skin tones. (See Neutral below). The tricky part is being certain that the undertone of the stocking blends with your skin, and often you don't get to know that until the package is opened and it is actually on the leg. When you find the right shade, stay with that brand so that you don't have to go through the trial-and-error process again (not to mention spending the money for something that doesn't work color-wise).

GRAYISH OFF-BLACK TO BLACK: Best with gray, black, and also possible with navy. Avoid beige tones with gray, black, and navy.

NEUTRAL: The best neutrals are those that blend with your skin tone. This is the shade to wear when you want your leg color to be as unobtrusive as possible. For example, a slinky **High Risk Red** dress makes enough of a statement without red stockings! Neutral hose would also be worn with white shoes.

VERY DARK AND VERY LIGHT STOCKINGS/TIGHTS: Trend colors (such as pastels), dark (such as **Maroon**), or bright opaques will change according to the latest fashion. The general guideline is to blend to your shoe color, but for a fun look, blend to a color in the top of your outfit.

9 Are there any rules for appropriate shoe and sock colors for men?

SHOES: Unless you are wearing white or light sneakers with really casual clothing, the best rule of thumb for business wear is a shoe that is darker than your pants. The best basics are black and brown, with colors like **Oxblood Red** (a deepened reddish brown) running a close third. This is the choice that is generally available in men's leather goods, such as briefcases and belts. Belts and shoes should match, again, to create a visual connection.

SOCKS: Most fashion authorities agree that a man's socks should match, blend, or relate to tie color. For example, a **Ruby Wine** and **Silver Gray** striped tie worn with **Maroon** socks. Bright red socks would be a bit much so a deep shade of wine is a better choice, yet it still remains within the red color family. Another example is a **Sky Blue** and **Light Taupe** tie worn with **True Navy** socks. **Sky Blue** is related to **True Navy** and light blue socks would really be geeky! Light socks give a casual look to an outfit, so they are not appropriate for business wear. You are always "safe" with darker sock colors. If you are not wearing a tie, socks should match the shoes.

10 Does white really "go with everything?"

There is no one definitive white that works with everything. Pure whites, as they are so clean and pristine, often have a bluish undertone, rendering them very cool-looking and appropriate to wear with clear, light, bright, mid, or deep cool colors. The warmer whites that lean more to cream work best with warm colors, again in light, mid, bright, or deep warm tones.

The salt and pepper of the fashion world, black and white can be done in either pure white and black or creamy white and black. A person with cooler skin looks best in the cool whites, while warmer-skinned people would find a creamier tone more in keeping with their skin tones. If you have difficulty discerning whether you have cool or warm skin, you are probably one of those people that have a bit of both and it's the slightly off-whites that look best on you.

A color purist might look for a blue black to wear with a pure cool white or a brown black to couple with cream. But this is truly splitting hairs, as most people can't really differentiate between those subtle nuances, and you would drive yourself crazy trying to find just the right "temperature" in black. As a result of varying undertones of black, such as blue or brown, for example, it is actually more difficult to put shades of black together than it is to combine black and white.

Combining whites is not a good idea. Putting a creamy white and a pure white together will make the off-white appear dingy when placed next to a pure white. As to the old "white-shoes-are-the-summertime-basic-that-goes-with-everything routine," that is really outdated. Unless you are wearing enough white in the outfit to visually support white shoes, as in white shirt, shorts, and sandals, or white shirt, white belt, khaki skirt, and white shoes, white will be a shining beacon that leads directly to your feet. If you have really shapely legs and want to show them off, white shoes will do it for you.

In reality, most women want to flatter their legs and not call too much attention to less than pretty feet or to heavy legs. In that case, a neutral color works best (See neutrals on page 48). As to white shoes worn with pants, that is never a problem as the length of the pant presents a longer line to the body and conceals the problem areas.

11

Are there any basic guidelines when buying cosmetic colors? I often like the way they look in the store and when I get them home, I don't like the way they look on me in "real life."

As every woman knows, it is easy to accumulate a drawer full of rejects, such as the makeup base that turned out to be the wrong shade and looked mask-like when applied to your face (as opposed to your trying it on your hand). Or the lipstick that looked great in the store display, but just didn't make it on your lips when you tried it at home. Expensive mistakes like this can add up—a lot of money can go down the lipstick tubes, so to speak.

Certain shades can look totally different on the skin than they do in the container, not only because of the way they look when actually applied but also because of a reaction to your body chemistry (oily skin, ruddy skin, sallowness, etc.). I recommend buying cosmetics only after they have been applied and left on the skin for a while, as in a demonstration. Check yourself in daylight as that will reveal mismatches, but if that is not immediately possible, at least under good clear lighting sources.

Don't be shy about telling the cosmetic salesperson that you don't necessarily want the latest, hottest trend color, but you do want the colors that will be most flattering. If you are like most people, you will try new colors but inevitably go back to your proven favorites.

COSMETICS HAVE been used throughout the ages for camouflage, concealment, or physical enhancement. Flattering cosmetic colors not only make you look wonderful, but they are also a great exercise in color creativity.

There is nothing wrong with that because you need to acknowledge your personal color comfort level, but you do want to avoid being caught in a time warp, and it is important to get some professional guidance from time to time. There is nothing that dates a woman more than continuing to wear the same lipstick color that she wore to her high school prom!!! On the other hand, don't underestimate your own good judgment. When a color on the face just looks odd, it's probably because it *is* odd!

Here are some color pointers for choosing your most basic cosmetics:

LIPSTICK AND BLUSH: If you have warm coloring, then the warmer colors are probably going to be your first choice. But if you wear some cool colors, such as a purple in the grape family, you will need a subtle cool color. If you have cool coloring, but have an affinity for pretty coral shades, then you will need a warmer-toned lip and cheek color when you wear those shades. If your coloring seems to be a combination of warm and cool tones, then you will need both shades as well. Some people simply can't handle vivid red, fuchsia, purple, and orange on lips and cheeks, no matter what the trend. Regardless of coloring, there is always a soft, natural "brownish" tone that works best as a basic color for people who simply don't want too much of a color statement on the lips for "every day."

If your lipstick turns bluish, no matter what you wear (as a result of acid in the skin), try a yellow or greenish undercoat to obliterate the blue tone.

ILLUSTRATION: CLAIRE SMALLEY, FROM PANTONE VIEW COLOUR PLANNER

MAKEUP BASE: One basic makeup color should blend with your skin tone. Match it as closely as possible so that you can't see a line of demarcation under the chin. Use a colorless, translucent powder over the makeup base so that it doesn't change color.

EYESHADOW COLORS: These can vary with several options. Choices include:

■ The color of the undertones in eyes, such as teal shadow with blue-green eyes, or amber with brown eyes.

■ A complementary color that intensifies the color of your eyes, such as taupe for blue eyes, or a soft grayish mauve to complement green eyes. (See color wheel, page 3)

■ Matching a shadow color to the color of the outfit, or an accessory color.

Whatever the choice, keep it subtle. If a color appears to be too vibrant, dust it down with some gray or taupe, if necessary, as it should shadow, not overshadow your eyes.

12 If you color your own hair or just want to know more about hair color, are there any general guidelines?

If you color your hair, choosing the right shade can be more confusing than choosing cosmetics. As a general rule, the hair-coloring shades tend to go in the three different directions that correspond with your skin and eyes: warm, cool, or some place in between that is often referred to as neutral. The name of the product will often give you a clear indication of the "temperature": Arctic Blonde is cool, Honey Blonde is warm, and Neutral Blonde is that in-between shade. The photo on the box is also a good indicator of the color inside. But if the names are somebody's flight of fancy, such as "Flirtatious Fawn" or "Bashful Beige," it's anybody's guess!

Body chemistry can affect hair just as it does cosmetics. It is possible that you have a natural red or gold tone that has a tendency to skew the color in that direction no matter what color you choose to use. This is not necessarily a bad thing, unless you want to play down that red tone. If that's the case, then deliberately choose a color that is meant to add cooler tones, such as ash.

Too much time in a chlorine-treated swimming pool can give your hair a slightly (or more than slightly) greenish tinge. Use a reddish tone to neutralize the green. If you are a blonde or have gray hair, especially if your coloring is warm, and you have used a product that has added too much violet or silver, a golden shade can be a good neutralizer. As you well know, if you have ever been in this predicament, strange things can happen to your skin tone if your hair coloring clashes. Hair is an important part of your self-image, so it is well worth your time to get the color right.

If all of this seems too confusing and/or involved, your local beauty supply can be a help, provided they have knowledgeable people available. All of the hair-coloring companies have web sites and information numbers available to you where you will get really helpful guidance. If you are still totally confused or have really made a mess of the color, then you need a professional hair colorist to undo the damage.

The best advice for hair coloring is that your natural hair color is never wrong, but if you want to change it, cover it up or simply enhance it, use the shades that will make it look most natural.

The following can be used as a guideline.

BLONDE

If you have cool coloring, such as alabaster or fair skin, or a blue undertone in dark skin and would like to be a cool blonde, then the ash or platinum tones will work best. A tinge of yellow is all right, but brassy gold just won't do it for you. You will want to eliminate as much gold as possible. Your best shades may be referred to as Ash, Nordic, Platinum, Cool Beige, Glacier, Moonlight.

If you have warm coloring or have a very light to deep golden undertone to your skin, then it is the warmer blonde tones that will flatter you most: Warm Blonde, Golden Blonde, Honey Blonde, Warm Beige, Amber, Caramel.

If you have difficulty discerning whether you are warm or cool, and cosmetic salespeople have a problem determining your undertone, then you are probably right in the middle, where either neutral or streaked hair tones that combine both warm and cool will look best on you.

REDHEAD

Although you would think all redheads would be in a warm category, actually there are different undertones in the skin of a redhead. A true auburn color has a relatively cool cast as opposed to the coppery undertones of a warm-skinned redhead. As a matter of fact, a redhead with sallow or yellowed skin should be cautious of overdoing warm tones, which may emphasize sallowness, so a mixture of auburn and coppery shades is often the best solution.

Red hair also has a tendency to become brassy, so some cool auburn undertones can help to keep the brassiness at bay. Again, a variation of color streaks in the hair can keep a better balance.

Cool-skinned redheads with very fair skin should look at shades such as: Sherry, Berry, Plum, Garnet; Light, Medium or Dark Auburn.

Warm-skinned redheads should look for products named Sun Bronze, Coppertone, Red Penny, Honey Red, Burnished Copper, Coppertone, Ginger Spice, Tawny Red, and if you are really brave, Feisty Pumpkin.

BROWN

Cool-skinned brown-haired people will usually have ash undertones that may range from very light to very dark. If a red tone is present in the hair, it is auburn or berry-colored. The names are often described as Light Ash Brown, Medium Ash Brown, Dark Ash Brown, Sable, Driftwood.

Warm-toned brown-haired people lean to the amber or honey tones. Again, the names are suggestive of warmth so they are easy to find: Light Warm Brown, Honey Brown, Golden Brown, Russet Brown.

The neutral tones that are variegated combinations of cool and warm undertones will look best in hair shades that are not easily definable as cool or warm, but could carry names such as Fawn, Medium Brown, Taupe, Tweed, Toasted Almond, Acorn Brown. They too look best with variegated streaks of warm and cool brown tones in their hair.

GRAY, SILVER, OR WHITE

At one point in time, little gray or white-haired ladies (and men, but they never would admit to it) put blue rinses in their hair. Hair coloring ads boasted the claim that they could "get the yellow out" as if it were a dreaded affliction. But if you have warm skin, a slightly warmer cast will look more natural. Remember that nature intended for your hair to blend with your skin and eyes. If your skin is a bit sallow or leans to olive, you might try livening up the gray by putting a rinse on it that will make it shiny rather than blue.

Cool rinses for silvery hair are easy to find with names such as Silver, Cool White, Icy White, or Silver Diamond. Warm gray rinses are harder to distinguish as they may have names like Pearly White or Moonlight, which could be warm or cool. The term "salt and pepper" describes those who are changing from their youthful dark hair color to a mixture of dark and light. Those with cool coloring will have pure white or silvery hair emerge, while those with warm skin will have a more "pewter" effect and not quite as pure a white. Those with more neutral coloring look best if they can keep the streaked variation of salt and pepper in their hair as it looks best with their variegated skin tones.

BLACK

Truly black hair always has a cool undertone appearing at times like an inky blue black. If you are of Asian descent, you might have this gorgeously glossy hair color. If you have warm, honeyed coloring, your hair will not be this bluish black. It might be very dark, but it is actually the darkest shade of brown or umber black, and that is why dyed blue-black hair can look so blatantly unnatural on some people. This is especially true for men, as they can't disguise their natural skin tone with cosmetics.

Blue-black hair is more difficult to retain in later years because it is so harsh next to a yellowing or aging skin. Dark, blue-black skin can also handle blue-black hair, while a cool dark ash brown will work best on "maturing" skins for people with fairer complexions.

The same principles of color apply to men as they do to women. If graying hair makes you feel older and you're just not ready for it, then by all means use the products available to you, but you have to make the commitment to keep it up regularly. Growth of the unwanted color will look obvious. Highlighting or variations of color are less obvious than a solid shade, as the new growth is not as apparent and you can go for a longer period of time without re-coloring.

Men really need to stay with more subtle colors, especially if they don't want the coloring to be noticeable. Dark blue-black Count Dracula-like looks are too severe on less than youthful skin. Don't try to turn the clock back to your high school hair color. For both sexes, hair color should be softened to de-emphasize changes in skin tone that inevitably come with the aging process.

13 What is the origin of khaki and why is it so popular?

The ubiquitous color of simplicity, informality, and "basic-ness": This tannish, often tinged with greenish, twill-like fabric is not the stuff ball gowns are made of. Although we might never call it glamorous, khaki has been glamorized over the years by stars of the silver screen. Katherine Hepburn, Greta Garbo, Clark Gable, and James Dean wore it, both on and off the set. Pat Boone wore it with his white bucks and button-down shirts. And today khaki graces the big screen as well as the small screen in practically every sit-com and in many commercials.

But, unlike tan, khaki is a rather exotic name. Where did it come from? We can thank a certain Punjab-based lieutenant, Harry Lumsden by name, an English chap who tore off his stifling, attention-riveting scarlet felt jacket to do battle in the comfy cotton pajamas that he had dyed the color of mud! Before long, his entire company of infantrymen were rifling through their trunks, pulling out their old pj's and dying them by using the same method—a colorant that came from a local plant called "mazari." The regiment was re-named the "mudlarks," and in typical British understatement, their commander stated of the newly invented khaki shade, "It's not a bad color for work!" Little did they know just how true that would be in the future.

When word spread of the radical departure from the usual military garb, there were various imitators who tried all manner of colorants: ink, coffee, tea, tobacco juice, and yet more mud. It wasn't until 1884, thirty-eight years after Harry began playing with mud, that khaki was patented as a colorfast dye. Currently, khaki is less a definitive single color than it is a variety of tints, tones, and shades—from dusty tannish tones such as **Pale Khaki**, **Boulder**, and **Putty** to light, mid, and deeper greenish casts, such as **Bog**, **Hemp**, and **Gravel**.

Born historically of wartime usage, from uniforms, battle fatigues, and Teddy Roosevelt's charge up San Juan Hill in his epauletted khaki bush jacket, to dashing wartime correspondents and the ubiquitous color of camouflage, today's khaki symbolizes more of the war of the workplace. What originated from battle and army fatigues has expanded to everyday issue.

But it's not just about khakis done in low-key sportswear anymore. Elegant designers like Ralph Lauren have lifted khaki to new heights of haute at higher prices, so that khaki may very well grace our walls, beds, windows, and floors, or cover our chair seats as well as our posteriors.

14 Why am I so attracted to specific colors for clothing?

Of the many environments that surround you, that of your clothing is the most personal. It is called your "intimate environment." As mentioned previously, most importantly, you choose clothing just as you do anything else in your environment—because you have an affinity for those colors and because they create a pleasing, confidence-building, and comfortable environment around you.

Contrary to what you might think, no one is totally clueless

PHOTO: CHICO'S RETAIL SERVICES, INC.

Many people feel comfortable in midnight blues and navies as these colors are flattering to a wide variety of skin, hair, and eye colors.

about color. A little careless sometimes, too reliant on other people's opinions, but I earnestly believe (and experience has taught me) that no one is entirely without any color judgment at all. So what you *sense* and *see* plays an important role in your wardrobe decisions, especially in terms of what you see in the mirror.

For example, if you have hair the color of burnished copper, one glance in the looking glass tells you how fabulous you look in **Ginger** red and **Golden Apricot**. If you are a man, you might lean to **Camel** and **Desert Sand**. And if your skin is sallow, no one should have to tell you to avoid **Bright Chartreuse**. You may have really good instincts about your personal colors. You have learned to read the reactions of others, and you know when your choices are validated by a favorable look or comment, or no comments at all and that can be even more telling. But please don't look for approval all the time—let your own good feelings and instincts guide you.

We do not choose color exclusively by what we see, but we also judge by what we feel. It is difficult to separate the two. Our emotional responses and the feelings that we have about color can sometimes override what we see. An astute salesperson might tell you that **Amber Yellow** is fabulous on you because you have tiny flecks of amber in your eyes, but if that tape recorder in your mind goes into instant replay and remembers your mother telling you that you should never wear yellow (because she disliked the color), you will eject that recommendation.

15 I usually gravitate to the colors I really like in clothing and accessories, but why do I still make costly mistakes?

There are several reasons, among them, persuasive advertising, current fads, and the bargains that are so hard to resist. Sales can be great for the budget, but the bargain that hangs ignored in the closet is no real bargain. We've all succumbed to that seemingly fabulous buy to find that in the cruel light of day the color was not only "off," it also was awful!

And then there are those well-meaning (most of the time) friends, spouses, and significant others who love to dispense their abundant advice. Good advice can be very helpful, but you must consider the source. Are they truly objective in the way they see you? If they are, you are lucky to have such wise and wonderful counsel. But remember that everyone carries around his or her own subjective color baggage, and it will color his or her thinking (literally).

Choosing a single favorite (or least favorite) color is not a problem for most people. Ask most people about their favorites, and they usually will respond very quickly with "I love blue" (or whatever color it happens to be) and "I detest bright orange." But colors are rarely used in isolation. Choosing one color that you really like is fairly simple, but combining that color with other hues, shades, tints, and tones can be a major challenge. If this is the part of color coordination that really intimidates you, the answers to many of the questions in this book will help guide you and give you greater color confidence.

And if color harmony comes quite naturally and effortlessly to you, you will validate how really smart you are!

16

What is the best way to combine colors so that they are flattering, yet look very personal and unique?

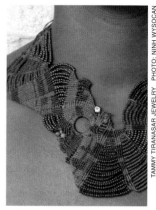

Everyone has a personal color signature that is created by wearing colors that repeat or enhance hair, skin, and eye color. By assembling these special shades you will create a core of colors that will have your own personal stamp. For example, if your hair is medium brown streaked with blonde tones and you have changeable chameleon-like eyes that range from blue to green and a rosy skin tone, wearing a tweed jacket that has flecks of brown and beige, a blue-green shirt, and a tie or scarf with those same colors and a touch of rose will create your own signature colors. These colors are truly you—a wonderful way to capitalize on your own coloring and make you stand out from the crowd.

Everyone has a personal color "signature" based on hair, skin and eye colors. Wearing accessories or clothing that repeat elements of your personal coloring will be flattering and distinctive and pleasing to others as well.

This doesn't mean that you wear exactly the same combination all the time as that would get stale, but it does mean that you have created a look that you can always depend on by varying the contrasts, patterns, and some of the colors themselves. An added plus is that you have created a wardrobe around colors that always coordinate. Trendy touches can always be added, such as a yellow-green shirt to substitute for the blue-green that will make your chameleon eyes look yellow-green. It's fun and a creative challenge to keep it fresh and updated.

This doesn't preclude the need for a navy blazer or a black power suit or any of the appropriate colors for different occasions, but it does create a comfort zone that you can always go back to, even if it's just in your favorite flannel robe or cozy oversized fleece sweater.

Here are some additional tips for selecting signature colors based on specific coloring:

- If you have hair, skin and eyes with very little contrast, such as very dark skin, eyes, and hair that appear almost black, there are actually other undertones present. Extremely dark skin and hair may appear to be blue-black. So a **Jet Black** or **True Navy** sweater and pants accented with an **Ultramarine** blue shirt and a touch of Pristine white to add sharp contrast (and enhance the white of the eyes) would look terrific.

- If your skin is a deep dark brown, a brownish black, such as **Black Coffee**, would look subtly striking. An **Emerald** green shirt would compliment the coffee-colored skin and a touch of **Winter White** would add the most flattering contrast to the deep warm shades.

- If your hair is silver, your eyes a light blue, and your skin is fair, there is nothing like the drama of **Jet Black**, **Ink Blue**, **Eggplant**, or **Charcoal Gray** worn with contrasting **Snow White** or **Silver Gray** and a truly vibrant touch of **Fuchsia Red**.

- Redheads, of course, by virtue of their unique coloring, can't help but attract attention. If you are a copper-toned redhead with cream-colored skin and amber eyes, you simply know that the very same shades are magical on you.

- Most Asian skin tones are flattered by complementary colors to the olive base in their skin. So reds such as **Rouge Red**, **Blush** pink as well as vibrant tones such as **Raspberry** or **Magenta** will reflect a healthy glow onto the skin. These shades will also flatter dark hair and dark eyes.

- Sandy-haired people with beige skin tones and brown eyes invariably go for the neutrals, especially in beige and beige-taupes. Although they are a reflection of your own coloring, if you wear them consistently and with very little contrast, you will disappear into the woodwork. Wear these classic

TAMMY TIRANASAR JEWELRY   PHOTO: NINH WYSOCAN

PHOTO: CHICO'S RETAIL SERVICES, INC.

THIS OUTFIT IS BOTH complimentary and complementary to the model. The balanced use of dominant **Blue Iris** and **Baltic** blue with subordinate accents of **Spicy Orange** and **Cadmium Yellow** are complementary to each other as well as the model's beautiful skin tone.

tones, but add a touch of contrast, something memorable, especially when on a job interview. Most likely you will lean to midtone, softer shades as your coloring is not dramatic. And that's fine if it fits your comfort zone. An uncomplicated **Simply Taupe** shade, for example, is wonderful with shades such as **Green Tea** to complement eyes and hair, and a dash of **Dusty Lavender** that can be highlighted on the lips and cheeks.

17 Is there a difference between the term "complimentary" (spelled with an "i") colors and "complementary" (spelled with an "e") colors?

Yes, there is a difference. A complimentary color is any color that is especially flattering to you. The dictionary definition is "something said to express praise and approval." So a complimentary color is definitely worthy of a compliment. A complementary (with an e) color is one that specifically contrasts (attractively) with your hair, skin, and eye colors. Again, as defined in the dictionary—"something that completes or perfects."

Complementary or contrasting color combinations are those directly across from each other on the color wheel. (See page 3 for a detailed description of the color wheel.) They are called complements because they complete each other.

Colors, left to right: **Blue Iris, Baltic, Spicy Orange, Cadmium Yellow, Jet Black**

Purple, for example, is the complement to yellow and never looks more purple than when it is next to yellow. This is the reason why a sandy blonde looks so terrific in shades of lavender or grape.

Blue complements orange and red complements green. In a patterned tie, **Rosewood** red and **Mosstone** green would be outstanding together. When used in the brightest intensities, complementaries provide instant dynamism and are real attention-grabbers. The complementary color effect is the reason why so many redheads wear green; although, in truth, blue is the true complement because redheads don't really have red hair—it is more akin to orange.

Complementary combinations can be used to advantage, but there are some pitfalls for personal coloring. If your skin flushes easily and you have a ruddy complexion, bright green will bring out the pink (light red) in your skin. The green should be lightened or deepened for a more flattering effect.

When the intensity of one or both of these complementaries is muted, the combination is much easier to view and far more subtle. For example, an **Azalea Pink** and **Pineneedle** green is less jarring optically than **Shocking Pink** paired with **Kelly Green**. You can soften the shock of complementaries by choosing appropriate shades and tints of these two hues.

When intense or strongly contrasting colors are offset by neutral colors, the combination becomes richer because the neutrals enhance the brighter colors by making them easier to view. For example, vivid **Skydiver** blue and **Bird of Paradise** orange might be great fun in a bathing suit or a Hawaiian shirt, but when these two hues are mixed with gray, beige, or taupe, the combination gains a degree of elegance and a quieter neutral shade to use as an accessory color.

Complementary colors can enhance personal coloring more effectively than any other combinations because they can alter the "fading" phenomenon that comes with aging. Our eyes get lighter with age, the hair is robbed of pigmentation, and the skin yellows (it's less depressing to liken it to fine lace than old newspapers!). Cosmetics and hair coloring can help considerably, but using complementary combinations can help as well

Blue eyes are enhanced by browns, oranges, cranberry, and corals. Green eyes are flattered by wines, pinks, and reds. Hazel eyes are chameleons that pick up and reflect many of the colors that are worn near them. This eye color contains many colors, but one shade usually dominates. Complementary colors are especially effective with hazel eyes and can virtually change their color.

Brown eyes and hair are complemented by greens, especially blue-greens. Since gray is a neutral, it really doesn't have a complementary color as such, but is enhanced by touches of color. Gray eyes are rare and closely akin to the palest blues or greens, so the colors mentioned above in those categories will be the most flattering. Black does not have a true complement, but both bright hues and white work well as contrast.

If you are a blonde, shades of purple and blue-purple will make you look blonder; and, as previously mentioned, although green flatters redheads, blue-greens and bright blues are even more effective. The signature colors on page 56 will also give you more suggestions for complementary colors.

18   Where should I look for color guidance in clothing/cosmetic choices?

You can learn a great deal about color by observing role models or others you admire in your personal life, in films, on television, in fashion magazines, catalogs, and/or advertisements. There are always new books full of information and illustrations to pore over. Some stores have personal shoppers on staff, and there are color/image consultants who can be helpful in giving you objective guidance on clothing choices.

As far as cosmetics are concerned, department stores, spas, and beauty salons are filled with knowledgeable cosmetic salespeople and/or makeup artists. All of these play an important part in your clothing and cosmetic decisions, but ultimately it's your own innate esthetic color sense—what you feel comfortable with and what you see, especially what you see in the mirror or mirrored in the eyes of others who respond and react to you—that will make the final color decision.

19   Are colors still limited by the season of the year?

Today all colors are considered "trans-seasonal." That is, they can span the seasons and are no longer limited to specific times of the year. It is truly the weight or look of the fabric that determines the season more than the color. For example, a diaphanous **Powder Pink** organdy dress would be more appropriate in spring and summer as its sheer fragile weight would not offer much wintertime warmth. But that same delicate **Powder Pink** in an angora sweater would be a welcome touch of springtime color to a dismal winter day, as well as other spring and summertime pastels such as **Viola**, **Pistachio Green**, or **Porcelain Blue**.

A typical fall color such as **Mandarin Orange** can be as wonderfully effective in a textured cotton shirt in summer as it is in a wool winter coat. Leather goods such as sandals, shoes, and bags in a color such as **Buckskin** and metal jewelry in shades such as **Copper Brown** have always been acceptable summer colors and have now crossed over into other textures as well.

There is always the question, "When is white appropriate?" Regardless of what the fashion magazines tell us about white shoes not being limited to the old time span of Memorial Day through Labor Day, white shoes on a slushy winter street would be pretty silly. White boots, they say, would work in winter, although you might look like you had on your mother's old go-go boots! So common sense should rule. If you live in a semi-tropical area such as Scottsdale, San Diego, or Miami, you can push the white-shoe issue beyond the two holidays mentioned. The weather and the geographical area should be your guide.

Evening wear for women has always crossed seasonal color boundaries, with colors such as dramatic **Fuchsia Pink** and **Ultra Violet** worn in summer as well as in the holiday season. Men's formal cummerbunds and ties are now available in a kaleidoscope of colors at every time of year. Even the traditional black-tuxedo-in-winter rule has been relaxed to include colors such as **Dove gray** or **Black Coffee**.

20 What is the best color plan for packing when going on a trip?

The key word is plan. Packing without a color plan and a written list is an invitation to wardrobe chaos when you get to your destination, no matter where that destination may be. Start with a calendar noting the days of your trip and note your activities on each day. Even if you don't know exactly what the activities will be—such as on a non-working vacation simply for relaxation—you know your destination, whether casual tropical or a ski resort, perhaps a large cosmopolitan city with opportunities to see shows and eat in great restaurants. It will simply remind you of what you should include in your bag should the opportunity arise.

Leave enough space to fill in all the necessary clothing: main garment plus socks/stockings, accessories, undergarments, and a jacket, sweater or other wrap for colder or air-conditioned destinations. Especially when going to a trade show, convention, or a meeting in a hotel, don't forget a layerable coordinated wrap, as the inside of meeting rooms is usually the temperature of a meat locker no matter where the city is located. When I do color seminars, I generally wind up in a frigid, cavernous, windowless room. One of the coldest destinations I go to is Las Vegas in summer, not Chicago in winter!

List everything else you will need for the trip: pajamas, slippers, bathing suit, etc. The pivotal color should always be a basic and it doesn't have to be black, although black is always a dependable place to start.

Depending on the length of the trip, your activities while there, and the ease of care of your clothing when you get there, a second basic may be necessary as well. For example, if **True Navy** is your basic, then **Silver Gray** might be your second basic. You would be able to wear the components of both colors together, perhaps gray pants and a navy shirt. A third and fourth color could be combined in a print or used as solid accent, possibly a solid **Crimson** red tie or a patterned tie that combines **Cardinal** red, **True Navy**, **Silver Gray**, and a touch of a deeper **Steel Gray**.

It's the lightweight accessories, blouses, shells, jewelry, ties, and non-bulky sweaters in the accent colors (such as the signature colors mentioned above) that will give you good alternatives to wear with the basics. They don't take up a lot of space, are lightweight, yet offer you some alternatives so that your basic scheme doesn't get tiresome, especially if you are going to be seeing the same people every day.

Check each item off as it is packed. Then you don't have to rely on your memory as that invariably results in rooting around in the bottom of the suitcase and making a big mess of everything that was so carefully folded and coordinated. The last thing to pack is the shoes, tucking them into the sides of the case. If your chosen basic is black, never take just one pair. Wear a pair of black shoes and pack a pair of black shoes. If your entire travel wardrobe revolves around the one pair of black shoes and your luggage is lost, or a heel comes loose, you are in trouble. Keep the list as it is a record of what you packed, should the luggage get lost.

The following is an example of a color plan for the traveling professional. Women may substitute a dress for slacks and a scarf or jewelry for the tie. It may seem like a lot of time spent on pre-planning, but it is well worth the fore-thought, as it will make the process effortless when you get to your destination.

SUNDAY, JUNE 30
Travel Day
True Navy casual cotton slacks
Kelly Green T-shirt
True Navy cotton belt
True Navy lightweight water-repellant jacket
True Navy loafers/socks

MONDAY, JULY 1
Business presentation 9 am – 4 pm
True Navy suit
Dapple Gray shirt
Cardinal red tie
True Navy belt
True Navy dress shoes/socks

**Cocktail reception in upscale restaurant
5 – 7 pm, Dinner 7 – 9 pm**
Change tie to pattern: navy, gray, red, and white
Change to navy silk shirt

TUESDAY JULY 2
**Touring plant with co-workers, lunch at plant
9 am – 1 pm**
Silver Gray Dockers
Silver Gray, **True Navy**, **Lemonade** checked shirt
True Navy loafers/socks

Afternoon free
Same outfit as morning

**Outdoor semi-casual reception
and dinner 6 – 10 pm**
Silver Gray slacks
Patterned shirt in silky texture, containing **Silver Gray**,
    True Navy, and other signature colors
True Navy belt
True Navy loafers
Lightweight **True Navy** sweater for cooler temperature

WEDNESDAY JULY 3
Attend seminar presentations 9 am – 4 pm
Charcoal Gray cotton slacks
Cardinal red knit shirt
True Navy belt
True Navy loafers/socks

**Dinner dance in hotel ballroom
7 pm – 11 pm**
True Navy suit
Silver Gray silk shirt
French Blue tie
True Navy belt
True Navy shoes/socks

THURSDAY, JULY 4
**Vacation day at beach 10 am – 6 pm
and fireworks at night**
Bathing suit - **Formula One** red, **Bright White**,
    and **True Blue**
Beach sandals
Pristine white cotton knit shirt
Pristine white shorts
Striped red, white, and blue cotton belt
    (in any of the above variations)

FRIDAY JULY 5
Return home
Same clothes as incoming trip

PHOTO: CHICCO USA, INC.

CHAPTER FOUR

Color and the Family

Color choices can

bring emotional

discord or harmony

to family spaces.

EVERYONE HAS QUESTIONS concerning the way family members relate and react to each other through color. Questions also arise regarding how family members react to the family pet, the family car, and special shared family occasions through color. Colorblindness will be covered, as it is a condition that plagues many families. Color choices can bring on some emotional family discord or harmony, depending on the situation. The following chapter addresses those questions that are constantly asked and, I hope, will be satisfactorily answered. Shared space brings its own special color problems and that is addressed in Chapter 6, "Decorating Your Home."

1 What is the best method of choosing appropriate colors for special parties and weddings?

Color is one of the most important elements of what makes a party special. Parties can be very emotional and meaningful life events, and color should be chosen with that same emotion, utilizing the colors that you really love and truly enjoy. I suggest that you look at the color quiz that you completed on page 23 and study your responses to the colors. Always go for one of your really positive responses.

For example, if **Opaline Green** is a color you have always loved (or newly discovered), then it simply speaks to you. Something special happens when you look at the color, and special is what these occasions are all about. Even if you don't consider yourself very color-aware, you will find a color, or colors, in the answers to that quiz that will have more meaning than any of the others. Once that choice is made, then the rest of the process is really not all that difficult.

Now go back to the color wheel on page 3 to help you with some inspiration for creating combinations. If the **Opaline Green** mentioned above were to be your dominant color, then an effective complement to that color would be in the red family for drama, or in the rose family for some subtlety. The mood of the color scheme will also be determined by the occasion. If this special occasion is to be a romantic dinner for two, a table setting with roses and candles and blush-colored champagne could inspire **Opaline Green**, **Veiled Rose**, and a bit of white **Pearl** for beautiful reflections. Using the information on page 3 you can work your way around the wheel to find the combination that suits your fancy and "speaks" to you.

One of the most emotional of all family occasions, weddings can be made even more beautiful by the use of the right color combinations that set the mood. Traditionally the bride gets to choose the colors. Ideally, she'll confer with everyone involved (including the groom) but in the final analysis, it is her day and she gets to choose. She will generally choose her favorite colors, unless there is a very domineering momma or momma-in-law. Since the wedding party needs to be dressed harmoniously, this is not really the time for individual choice. Again, it's the bride's call unless she defers to the other leading ladies. Usually, harmony ensues and we can only hope they will all live happily ever after. Coordinating the clothing, flowers, and table linens is well worth the effort when, in the years to come, the photos help you to remember the beauty of that special day.

Formal occasions and weddings are perfect for effective monochromatic combinations. At weddings, the bridesmaid or mother of the bride (usually) doesn't want to upstage the bride, yet wants to look elegant and special. Monochromes are the perfect solution to this need.

2 Has white always been the traditional color for brides?

In many cultures, brides have worn white for centuries to symbolize purity, chastity, and innocence. This was a tradition started by the ancient Greek brides, who went a step further and painted their entire bodies white and wore white flowers in their hair. In the 16th century, pale green was worn by young brides in Northern Europe and England to symbolize new life and the hope for fertility. This continued until Elizabethan times when the tradition of white as symbolic of all that is pure, young, and virginal began. However, even then white was still not the absolute choice for all brides.

From Elizabethan times to the rule of Queen Victoria, wedding gowns could be any color. They were most apt to be the bride's best dress in colors like burgundy, dark green, brown, and even black, especially if the groom was a widower and the bride was not exactly of blushing age. But Victoria favored white and the tradition started with her marriage in 1840. Godey's *Lady's Book*, the *Vogue* magazine of its day, stated that white "is the emblem of the purity and innocence of girlhood and the unsullied heart she now yields to the chosen one." Pretty flowery prose, but women in those days were "yielding" their hearts along with their dowries. With the Industrial Revolution and the coming of department stores in the 1890s, almost every woman aspired to a new white gown.

The Dutch also favored green, as depicted in the famous Jan van Eyck painting "Portrait of Giovanni Arnolfini and his Wife." In China, red was the favored color for weddings as it symbolized a healthy marriage filled with good fortune. But more recently many young brides of Asian background are emulating Western ways and have discovered the more romantic aspect of wearing white for weddings.

There is an old English poem that tells of what might befall a bride depending on the color of her dress:

Marry in white, you will have chosen all right.

Marry in gray, you will go far away.

Marry in black, you'll wish yourself back.

Marry in red, you'll wish yourself dead.

Marry in blue, you will always be true.

Marry in pearl, you'll be in a swirl.

Marry in green, ashamed to be seen.

Marry in yellow, ashamed of the fellow.

Marry in brown, you'll live out of town.

Marry in pink, your spirits will sink.

Obviously, modern brides pay little attention to most of these scary prophecies; nevertheless, many have gone back to the traditional white gown.

ALTHOUGH THERE ARE A VARIETY of colors modern brides might choose for their wedding dresses, many still opt for traditional whites, but may add uniquely colored trim and accessories for a very nontraditional touch.

PHOTO: MARLENA BIELINSKA   GOWN AND VEIL DESIGNED BY CHRISTOS

3 Is it true that "older eyes" start to perceive colors differently and, if so, at what age?

IMAGE PROVIDED COURTESY OF PANTONE, INC. © PANTONE INC. 2003

At approximately age 65 (and that is an average) there is a gradual yellowing of the lens of the eye. It is referred to as the "ginger-ale affect." This is not to be confused with cataracts, and not everyone is affected at exactly the same time or in the same way. As the yellowing descends over the eye, it is the cool colors, blue, blue-green, green, and blue-purple that are most affected. They will appear somewhat "murky" and not clearly defined, especially when used in combinations with each other.

A solution for this phenomenon is using warm colors or cool

VIBRANTLY COLORED or contrasting dishes and glassware are highly recommended for "older eyes" as the objects are easier to see. Older people are often finicky eaters, and strong color contrast and bright colors stimulate their appetites.

tones that are vibrant and cleaner. Another solution is to divide the cool colors by using a "buffer" color between them such as a neutral or contrasting warm shade. This is especially important in areas that could possibly be hazardous for seniors. For example, if a chair leg is blue and the carpet is blue-green, the line of definition could blur causing an older person to trip on the leg of the chair when passing. Steps may also be hazardous and further exacerbated by waning depth perception. Contrasting stair treads or a warm-colored runner would be a solution.

It is also advised that very dark flooring not be used as older eyes see this as a "bottomless pit" that makes them feel very insecure when stepping into that space.

Another important usage of color for the elderly is in "way-finding," a term that says exactly what it means—a method of identifying a pathway that will lead them in the right direction. This is helpful in large facilities such as hospitals or other public buildings they may frequent. And if they are living in assisted-care facilities or larger homes for the aged, using identifying colors in special activity rooms is very helpful as it will help to identify their destination.

Product packagers should be especially aware of the solutions mentioned in the second paragraph above. People are living longer lives, and those older eyes are still very viable consumers evaluating the products on the shelves. The directions on the labels, especially medicinal products, should be legible and clearly defined, color-wise. There is the potential for the older consumer to misread the instructions and put them back on the shelf out of sheer frustration, or worse than that, misread the instructions and over-medicate.

Naturally, sufficient lighting is always an issue in viewing colors as poor lighting can cause visibility or misinterpretation problems beginning as early as age 50. So it is not only the senior citizens who are affected, but the aging boomers as well.

4

Do babies really cry more in yellow rooms?

And do people really get more irritable in yellow surroundings?

These are two of the more ludicrous of color "factoids" having no basis in fact. As a matter of fact, most people associate yellow with sunshine, warmth, and cheer, and it is a mood enhancer, rather than a source of irritation. I have recommended yellow as a wonderful substitute for sunshine in geographic areas where there isn't a lot of sun in winter. (See SAD Syndrome, page 111). I have used the happy hue in my own home in the Northwest for just that reason and have always had positive response to the color from friends and visitors. They often come away with a commitment to use yellow in their own homes as it is so warm and welcoming.

As to babies crying more in yellow rooms, there are no studies that I can find to back that up. My own babies were raised in yellow bedrooms as it was a non-gender specific color in the days before we knew of the baby's sex prior to birth. They definitely had their irritable moments, but neither was a chronic crybaby.

So, if you love the idea of a delicious buttery yellow surrounding you and your family, by all means use it and see how sunny your dispositions will be!!

5

What is the origin of blue for boys and pink for girls?

The history of pink for girls and blue for boys is not altogether clear, as it springs from folklore that can change with the cultural origin. But the consensus is that in most cultures, blue is considered a protective color and since boy babies were valued more than girl babies, they were dressed in blue. Girls, according to old European folktales, sprang forth from soft unfolding pink roses. Similarly, in many cultures, the feminine role was associated with ruffles, sentiment, and nurturing, while the masculine side with earning a living in steadfast, laboring blue.

As roles, for the most part, are changing, it seems silly to adhere to outdated concepts. Although there are many other non-gender specific colors for infants, such as **Hushed Green**, **Tender Yellow**, **Fair Aqua**, **Ecru**, **Bleached Apricot**, or **Whisper White**, old traditions die hard, especially when the color quickly identifies the sex of the child.

UNISEX COLORS can start at a very early age. Although the subject matter of this charming mural may seem more typically feminine, the colors would be equally at home in a baby boy's bedroom.

PAINTING: ERIKA PARO

If you are a parent, you know that referring to a cherubic little girl as a boy can be really insulting to many new moms and dads. So you tape a tiny pink bow on the top of the fuzzy (or hairless) little head. And somehow it's even worse to call a baby boy a girl. Can't they tell this adorable little chunk is destined for stardom with the Dallas Cowboys? Put him in blue overalls, and no one will ever make that dreaded mistake again!

6 Are newborn boys and girls born with a different sense of color?

There is no hard evidence that proves that boy babies respond any differently to color than girls do. Infants of both genders see the contrast of dark and light before they see color. However, when color is placed in their line of vision, it will immediately capture their attention. If you are wondering how researchers would know this, as the teeny subjects can't be questioned, there are "eye tracking" studies that show that it is the primary hues of red, blue, and yellow that will instantly pull an infant's attention.

When the little tykes start to make color decisions for themselves, it's all about a very visceral reaction to the color, choosing what is most appealing. But as soon as they get a little older and start to interact with other little people, they may be tempted to emulate what their friends like. Even at a tender age, the mimicking behavior can begin, unless they are the leaders (sometimes the "bosses") whom other kids will copy.

Ultimately, they are influenced by parents' comments about a specific color, TV shows, or commercials, video games, favorite video, or film characters or important books. Traditionally, the blue-for-boys and pink-for-girls thing continues on in packaging and displays in stores in addition to the entertainment areas named above. However, the gender specificity is going through some major changes. A Nintendo character, Kirby, is a Pepto-Bismol pink, and it is aimed at both sexes. As more daddies wear pink or lavender shirts, you can be sure that the little ones will want to model themselves after a significant role model. That is, until they get to be opinionated 'tweens or teens when they don't want to do anything as dismally uncool as Dad does, which may or may not include the colors male adults wear.

Purple has certainly seen some significant gender specific changes in the last 10 to 15 years. Once considered to be feminine, more boy toys and action characters have sported purple clothes. Interestingly, more guys of all ages are wearing purple than ever before as a result of the sporting goods and sportswear industries that help to entice guys into purple through the graphics on skate boards, skis, and other adrenaline-pumping sport activities.

ILLUSTRATION: JANE BUTLER

ALL CHILDREN, 'tweens through teens, need their "space," and most importantly, should have the freedom to choose their very own personal color favorites.

7 Are women better at choosing colors than men?

From the beginning of time women have been the gatherers of berries, nuts, fruits, roots, and herbs, while men were the hunters and warriors. As a result, social anthropologists tell us that women have always been more visually attuned to color since it was the women who were responsible for seeing that the food was fresh and edible. Obviously color plays a very important part in food selection, not only for the aesthetics, but also for our very existence. A rotten blackened fruit was not a big deal, but a putrid purple root could do the whole tribe in!!

This ability to discern color was passed on through thousands of generations. In addition, when societies became more civilized and clothes evolved from loincloths to long dresses, it was the women who traditionally selected the fabrics, chose the colors, and became the seamstresses. It was also the women's role to decorate and outfit the home, and to oversee the garden. Woman's work was, for the most part, very color-related.

And when Momma went shopping, it was the daughter who usually accompanied her to

ILLUSTRATION: JANE BUTLER

ALTHOUGH MANY WOMEN have a natural affinity for decorating and selecting colors, there are many men who are equally talented in selecting the appropriate colors for the home.

observe what Momma did and the selections she made. Little girls were encouraged to dress their dollies and decorate their dollhouses, while little boys were encouraged to do the manly things like aggressively competing in sports or tinkering with their bikes (in preparation for the time they would do the same with their cars).

When cosmetics and hair color came into popular usage, it was also the woman who was the major consumer. As far as women are concerned, this proclivity to color was not only natural, but a skill that was honed through many years of observing the previous generation at the dressing table or having an aunt who was an Avon lady. This is not to say that all men lack talent in color selection. We can certainly look at some of the great male artists, both fine and commercial, as well as at fashion, interior, and theatrical designers throughout history who were celebrated for their skilled and often colorful work. So we can't overdo this Venus and Mars thing by saying all women are better at color selection than men. Regardless of gender, much of it depends on their innate talents and/or willingness to learn.

I have a friend who is married to a very left-brained engineer. She always chose his clothes and the colors because that's the way it had always been done in his family. He had always considered himself non-creative as he was never given the opportunity to choose colors for anything. His wife and mother did it for him. Eventually they bought a house with space for a sizable garden that he planned very methodically, plot by plot. His wife encouraged him to exercise the other side of his brain and do some creative color planning (as well as planting), and his newly developed skill with color arrangements from the garden literally blossomed.

8 Why do some men have trouble with color when shopping for clothing?

All men are not clueless about color. Those who are simply do not see color as a top priority. For them, clothing is all about comfort. They have that hunter-gatherer proclivity hard-wired into their DNA. They didn't have to look at the colors of the nuts and berries as women did to be certain they were edible. Mr. Neanderthal's job was to prowl around for a likely dinner in the form of an unsuspecting animal, no matter what the color.

When men shop for clothing with a female companion, they are most likely listening to what she has to say as they know they need the help. If they have learned their lessons well when they have gotten advice about color, they are likely to repeat those same colors in future shopping trips. Color trends are far less important to men than to women, but they will buy trend colors if a knowledgeable person recommends them, male or female.

Most men are simply not raised to think very much about style and color. For the most part, the thought of deliberately buying a red shirt because it is a sexy color doesn't enter into their realm of consciousness (well, most men). They are inclined to view fashion as a spectator sport and less as reality.

However, some of the mainstream magazines, TV shows, commercials, and films can have a positive influence. If they see the celebrities, sports figures, and musicians they admire wearing certain colors and styles and/or a favorite designer's line fits their image and comfort level, they will often want to emulate the look.

When Professor Henry Higgins of *My Fair Lady* fame grumpily asked, "Why can't a woman be more like a man?" he might easily have reversed the question—at least as far as shopping for color is concerned.

9 What causes colorblindness and how is it diagnosed?

Colorblindness is the inability to distinguish some or all colors. Most color deficiencies result in a limited ability to see shades of red and green, while others are completely colorblind to red and green, seeing both colors as shades of yellow. In a rare genetic defect of the retina (a condition called achromatopsia), those who are totally colorblind can see only shades of gray, white, and black. There is also a form of colorblindness that comes as a result of a degenerative disease of the eyes. Interestingly, alcoholism can lead to this condition as well.

Most colorblindness is an inherited sex-linked characteristic transmitted through females, affecting many more men than women. Statistically, about 8 percent of men and 0.5 percent of women have difficulty distinguishing colors. So the stereotype of the man perennially wearing mismatched socks is too true, unless he has a wife, significant other, or girlfriend to check him out before he leaves the house. Generally the problem of choosing the correct colors to wear together can be easily overcome by shopping with a cooperative female, an image consultant, or in a store with qualified help.

ALTHOUGH MOST MEN do not see clothes shopping as an enjoyable experience, they do enjoy the confidence that comes from wearing image-enhancing styles and colors.

PHOTO: COURTESY OF PAUL FREDRICK MENSTYLE

For the single guy or the man who travels a great deal, a list or labeling system can be an efficient remedy that helps to eliminate guesswork. Again, it does take a cooperative friend or family member to do the labeling or construct a list of what goes with what that is posted in or near the closet. A numerical system can be devised so that all pieces labeled with specific numbers can be worn together.

Many people, both male and female, have difficulty differentiating between really dark shades such as navy or charcoal and black, but this has more to do with poor lighting than visual acuity. If this is a problem for you, a huge help is keeping socks and stockings (the biggest challenge) separated into labeled containers or drawers.

It is also best to keep all items such as sweaters of same or similar colors in separate folded stacks on shelves. Similarly, all hanging items in the closet should be kept in color families. The color name can be written on the clothes labels with permanent ink so that the colorblind person knows where to put the garment after it has been worn or cleaned. This is a greater problem for smaller things, such as socks without an inside tag, but a small fabric tag marked with the color name, similar to those purchased for kids going off to camp, could be sewn inside these items.

Some colorblind or color-deficient people report that they are more sensitive to texture and shape than the person with normal color vision as they have learned to rely on those cues. If they are involved in creative fields such as architecture, design, or art, they place a great deal of importance on balance, contrast, form, and texture, which can certainly add an interesting dimension to their work. So perhaps they should not be labeled as "color-defective," but rather as "color-different!"

10   How well do animals and birds see color?

At one point in time, it was believed that some groups of animals were colorblind, seeing only shades of gray. But studies done in the 1990s showed that at least dogs, though partially colorblind, are not totally blind to color. It seems that they can tell red from blue and can even see differences in shades of blue and violet. Just as with partially colorblind humans, dogs cannot distinguish yellow, green, and orange. If you should have a pet pig, cat, or squirrel, experiments reveal that they exhibit the same kind of color vision.

Horses, sheep, and guinea pigs can see an even broader spectrum than dogs and cats. Chimpanzees are said to have color vision at least as good as humans, while many types of monkeys have an excellent sense of color, but at the same time prefer blue over red.

Some animals have even taken to painting to express their moods. Ruby, a talented elephant at the Phoenix zoo, unfortunately now deceased, started to paint rather expressive abstract art after she was encouraged by her keepers to pick up the brushes. In observing her behavior they believed that Ruby preferred bright colors on sunny days, but used more somber colors when the skies were overcast. To further demonstrate their beliefs about Ruby's observation and use of color, they said that in her compositions she was likely to use a dominant color worn by an observer who was watching her paint.

As color plays an important part of their behavior, it is believed that many types of birds and fish have good color vision. A male robin will defend its territory against any bird exhibiting red feathers, even if the feathers are on a dummy masquerading as another red bird. Birds are most attracted to red flowers and fruits, except for the Australian bower bird who prefers blue and will look for any tiny bit of blue it can find to

PHOTO: COLLAR BY DUNITZ & COMPANY, INC.

ALTHOUGH THIS BEAUTIFUL POOCH might have some difficulty in discerning her favorite colors, consumer studies have shown that pet owners enjoy enhancing their pet's appearance by choosing pet accessories in their animal's most flattering colors.

beautify its nest, from paper plates to blue berries or other blue scraps. It will even attack blue-feathered birds and pull the feathers out to support its rather aggressive decorating habits.

Fish are ambivalent about red. Some fish are greatly attracted by red while others totally avoid it. Vividly colored reef fish differentiate food and mood by color. Deep-water fish often respond only to blue, while sharks are greatly attracted to a color that marine biologists call "Yum-Yum" yellow. So you should leave your yellow bathing suit home the next time you swim in the ocean.

Generally speaking, the more colorful the species, the better the color vision. So it is believed that peacocks and parakeets see better than mice and men.

COLOR AND THE FAMILY

11   How does cultural background affect a person's reaction to color?

Cultural background and upbringing can definitely cause specific reactions to color, both positive and negative, and they are often passed on from one generation to another. This is especially true if you were raised in a very tight family unit or social system where there are rigid color restrictions. If a person's social sphere is limited or traditions are unquestioned, the color traditions and taboos will continue.

However, when people move from one type of social structure or location to another, enter a larger mainstream population, or climb up the economic ladder, they become more acculturated, and they will often shed some of the old beliefs and traditional mindsets about color.

An example of this type of change can be demonstrated within the Hispanic population of a large urban area such as Los Angeles, where there is a rich heritage of vibrant colors that emanates from Mexico. When someone emigrates from that country and lives within a largely Hispanic community and/or family, there is a certain comfort level in using colors that are indigenous to the country of their origins. But in the second and third generations, where there is more assimilation in schools, work, and social life, as well as the adaptation of colors seen on TV, in videos, films, shopping malls, and on the web, the more traditional colors are most likely replaced by the latest trend colors.

In the past, black would have been the rigidly prescribed symbol of death and mourning for widows, whereas today, black jeans are the ultimate sign of cool urban chic to a young fashion-forward teen of Hispanic background. If you were to visit Mexico, you would see this same sort of change happening in the larger urban areas where there are more worldwide influences being felt as a result of exposure to the entertainment world and to the use of the Internet. Generally speaking, the farther removed from large urban centers, the greater the use of traditional color.

When I visit areas of the world today to deliver seminars or work with clients, I am aware that the younger or more fashion-aware people are looking more and more similar. There has definitely been a movement to this international look, but we can only hope that traditional colors don't completely disappear in years to come. It's the diversity that enriches our outlook on color and enables us to better appreciate its origins.

12   Is it true that your car color and style preference are a reflection of your personality?

There is no question that the vehicle you drive is an extension of your personality—an unspoken, but clear message to the rest of the world. The message does not have to indicate the person you perceive yourself to be. It can also enable you to live out your fantasy and convey a message of who you would *like* to be. One of my former clients was the CEO of a large insurance company. He drove a sedate, low-key silver gray vehicle that looked like many other cars in the parking lot of his company, and it wasn't even a Jaguar, Mercedes, or Lincoln Town car! As soon as he retired, he bought the car of dreams—a vintage red Mustang in a perfectly polished, high gloss **Fiery Red**. He says he feels revitalized when he gets behind the wheel. It's brought back the energy and dynamism of his youth—a small price to pay for all that excitement and fulfillment of a lifelong fantasy.

PHOTO: BRUCE DALE PHOTOGRAPHY

THE LOVE AFFAIR WITH THE CAR begins for most people at a very early age and by the time they reach their teens, they fantasize about the kind of car they want to drive and, most importantly, the color of their "dream car."

Red is always the color that most people identify as sexy. It doesn't take much imagination to figure out why a low-slung red Porsche that has the ability to dart in and out of traffic with tremendous ease is identified with someone who wants to be imbued with all the sexy characteristics. In addition, red is the color that is always identified with high energy and speed. It's an aggressive color that doesn't just *command* attention, it *demands* attention. How can you ignore anyone in a red sports car? Your co-workers might see you as the mild-mannered Clark Kent when you work in a cubicle, but when you get into that hot little high-powered red sports car you *are* Superman (or Superwoman)!

No matter how much we try to buy a car strictly on its merits and mileage, unless you are totally color-blind, color is an important part of the equation, especially when it comes to wish fulfillment. We muse over the car we would buy if we won the lottery, and when we dream about that special car, the dreams are in living color.

No matter how you might rationalize that school bus yellow is the safest color to drive as a soccer mom with a car full of kids, if yellow just doesn't fit the image of who you think you are, you won't buy yellow. No matter what the trend might be in the latest car colors, if it's a color you can't tolerate, chances are you won't buy it. That's why, unless auto manufacturers are real trendsetters willing to take a big gamble, your selection is really rather limited to the "safer," proven salable colors.

Automakers should remember that Mom makes more than 60 percent of the car-buying decisions, and the family car is usually her car. It's now referred to as "the family room on wheels," providing a chat room, an entertainment center, a place to eat, drink, change clothes (or diapers), do personal grooming as well as functioning as communication central. It is truly one of the major areas where families gather. Although Mom is very concerned about safety features, practicality, economy, and size, the "look" and the color of the auto remain important attributes. This is true for many dads as well.

Someday, we have been promised, customization and technology may reach a level where colors, interior and exterior, will be changed at the flip of a switch. Currently, the interior styling often rivals the color on the outside. Beautiful leathers or look-like leathers come in luxurious shades that rival an expensive living room sofa. Metallic finished dashboards rival beautifully crafted giftware or jewelry. All of this comfort is more than window dressing when you consider that today's commuter spends an average of 82 minutes a day behind the wheel, more than double the time spent in the '80s.

So, if you had the perfect car in the perfect color, what would it be? Read on to find out what your choice of a car color says about you.

WHAT YOUR CAR COLOR SAYS ABOUT YOU

Vibrant Red:	Sexy, speedy, high-energy, and dynamic	**Dark Blue:**	Credible, confident, dependable
Deep Blue-Red:	Some of the same qualities as red, but far less obvious about it	**Deep Purple:**	Creative, individualistic, original
		Neutral Gray:	Sober, corporate, practical, pragmatic
Orange:	Fun loving, talkative, fickle, and trendy		
		White:	Fastidious
Sunshine Yellow:	Sunny disposition, joyful, and young-at-heart	**Black:**	Empowered, not easily manipulated, loves elegance, appreciates classic
Yellow Gold:	Intelligent, warm, loves comfort and will pay for it		
		Silver:	Elegant, loves futuristic looks, cool
Dark Green:	Traditional, trustworthy, well balanced		
		Taupe:	Timeless, basic, and simple tastes
Bright Yellow-Green:	Trendy, whimsical, lively		
Light to Mid Blue:	Cool, calm, faithful, quiet	**Deep Brown:**	Down-to-earth, no-nonsense

13 Do red cars really get more speeding tickets?

Yes, it's true that red cars, according to insurance and police department reports, do get more speeding tickets. Obviously, as mentioned in Question #12, red attracts and commands attention, not so much from the color standpoint but because the driver of the car feels more exciting behind the wheel of a red car. Excitement can be a heady, powerful experience, and a lot of that power can go directly to the accelerator!

You should know that all red cars are not equal speeding ticket magnets. The blue-reds are more toned done—it's the warm orangy reds that are all revved up.

14 Has color always been significant in religious symbolism?

Color has a long history of symbolic meaning in many religions. In early Christianity, the heavenly Trinity was blue for God, the Father; yellow for God, the Son; and red for God, the Holy Ghost. Heaven was blue, Earth was yellow; and hell, of course, was red as were depictions of Satan. Yet at the same time, red represented martyrdom. Green was Mother Nature—everlasting and faithful. Gold and yellow were power, glory, and splendor. Blue was hope, peace, sincerity, and serenity. The Virgin Mary was most often depicted in blue. Purple was endurance, penitence, and suffering. Many orders of nuns wore purple and rosaries often contained amethyst stones. White was chastity, simplicity, and purity. Nuns were married to the church in white, while black represented death and regeneration, two seemingly opposite themes, yet symbolic of both a beginning and an end.

In Kabalism, an ancient form of Judaism, color symbolism was significant. Colors carried many of the same meanings to several cultures and religions, such as the Egyptians, Babylonians, Assyrians, Greeks, Shintos, Confucians, Persians, and Druids. The concentration of divine light was white. Black represented understanding because it absorbed all light. This may be a clue to the connection between black and sophistication, since to be sophisticated is to be wise through experience. Wisdom was gray, a combination of white and black. Mercy was blue, strength was red, and beauty was yellow. Victory was green, signifying the combination of mercy (blue) and beauty (yellow). Glory was orange, combining strength (red) and beauty (yellow). Strength (red) and mercy (blue) led to the foundation of purple—the basis of all that is.

Many of these ancient meanings are still attributed to colors. They are passed on from generation to generation, and certain meanings seem contradictory. For example, black is associated with death, but also with sophistication. Yet the meanings remain similar in that black is seen as mysterious—whether the eternal mystery of death or the mystery of the sophisticated woman in black.

ONCE THOUGHT OF as a color for little old ladies, lavender has lost its gender and age-specific connotations.

PHOTO: COURTESY OF PAUL FREDRICK MENSTYLE

15 Is lavender still considered a color for little old ladies?

For many years, prior to the development of sophisticated and subtle hair coloring, little white-haired ladies "enhanced' their tight curly perms by applying bluing to their heads. This laundry-based product was generally used to make clothing appear a crisp white. Hair, however, is not the same texture as clothing, so the hair reacted by turning lavender. When technology enabled women to tinge their white hair to a more beautiful and lustrous silvery cast, bluing was no longer used. Today the little young ladies are more apt to have lavender hair than their stylish grandmothers.

Lavender's image as a specific female color changed in the 1980s as a result of the popular TV show "Miami Vice" that depicted a tough Miami detective, Don Johnson, sporting lavender shirts, proving that real men could wear lavender.

16

Does intense pink really make men (and boys) weak?

I can't tell you how many times I have been asked this question, especially from mothers of teenage sons! Actually there have been studies done that both prove and disprove this theory. The first study, and the most famous as it received a great deal of media attention, was conducted by Dr. Alexander Schauss of Tacoma, Washington. He observed that after a period of "hyper-excitement" his blood pressure, pulse, and heart beat lowered more rapidly when he viewed a specific shade of intense pink.

He felt that it might have an effect on human aggression and tested the theory at the Naval Correctional Center in Seattle. An admission cell was painted a vibrant pink, called Baker-Miller pink in honor of the doctors who allowed the theory to be tested. It was, in the event that you would like to try it, the color of Pepto-Bismol!

New confines were admitted to the cells and observed for 15 minutes during which time no incidents of radical behavior were recorded. The effects of the color lingered on for about 30 minutes after their removal from the cell. Many people, including myself, were surprised to find that the pink that was used was somewhat bright, and not at all docile. Some of my more skeptical colleagues felt that pink is still pink after all, the color of valentines, love, and icing on the birthday cake, so that it should follow that pink subdued the inmates and turned down the testosterone level.

Dr. Schauss felt that "the effect of Baker-Miller pink is physical, not psychological or cultural" and that people could absorb information through radiant energy sources and transmit that energy to the hypothalamus as well as the pineal and pituitary glands. In other words, you may also "see" with your glands.

Subsequent studies did not arrive at the same conclusions. Perhaps someone will revive the study and test it on a large enough group to really determine if some shade of pink really does make hyperactive males weak. If it does, it would make a great color for prison uniforms (or teenage boys' bedrooms!).

University studies done later tested the suggestibility factor of pink. What would happen if both men and women were tested? The researchers told a group of young men that they would become weaker when they viewed pink. They tested them by having them squeeze a dynamometer (those grip machines that test physical strength at carnivals). Then they tested a group of women in the same way.

The results of the test showed that the men responded by, in fact, becoming weaker, while the women became stronger. The women resisted the concept of stereotypical pink making them weaker. Maybe the real outcome of this study proves that men are more prone to suggestion than women!

PHOTO: DON PAULSON

CHAPTER FIVE

Color and Health

The health-giving

properties of color

in food have been

scientifically proved.

LIVING IN AN AGE of alternative therapies, holistic remedies, and a newer, more enlightened view of nutrition, we seek to heal ourselves physically, mentally, emotionally, and spiritually. We strive to keep our bodies and psyches in balance. Color can be a powerful provider of guidance and insight that helps us achieve that balance.

The health-giving properties of color, in food as well as the environment, have long been acknowledged. Colored lighting, color therapy, and color in health-care settings are all critical areas for exploration and enlightenment.

Whether proven by science or inspired by spiritual quest, encouraged by the power of suggestion, or the result of deeply imbedded memories, there is no question that color's effects are imprinted indelibly within the human psyche and spirit.

1 Can colored light or liquid be used for healing purposes?

Throughout history, amulets, gemstones, insects (dead or alive), flowers, feathers, dyes, and scores of other natural objects and substances have been thought to have special restorative powers based on their color. But the most fascinating to mystics, healers, shamans, scholars, and scientists alike have been those techniques that literally or figuratively bathe the body with colored lights and/or colored liquids.

Historically, people who dealt specifically with colored lighting (chromotherapists) were looked upon with skepticism in this country because many were associated with quackery. Today there is more acceptance of chromotherapy, and there are many accepted forms of colored-light treatment used by the medical profession. Researchers are becoming more open to the concept that many aspects of our mental and physical health are affected by the intensity, duration, and color of the light to which we are exposed.

Sophisticated diagnostic tools are available through the infrared thermograph, which can locate disease and injury with a scanning camera. Since each part of the body has a different temperature range, each is recorded as a color. When the thermograph records changes from the norm, the source of the problem can be pinpointed. More recently, highly evolved scanning techniques and computer technologies have been developed. For example, after injecting a patient's vein with colored dyes, the diagnostician can trace and pinpoint specific abnormalities that are immediately discernible on the computer screen.

For many years, premature infants with jaundice have been treated under blue lights that penetrate the skin. Ultraviolet lights are used to clean the air of operating rooms. Black light is used to treat psoriasis and red light for the treatment of migraines. Zapping lasers are being used in a variety of ways, from hair and wrinkle removal to more intricate cosmetic surgery. Biofeedback techniques utilize blue lights as a calming influence in stress reduction.

John Ott, one of the world's leading experts on lighting, devoted years of research to help bring about full-spectrum fluorescent lighting that closely duplicates natural sunlight. Sunlight itself has been used as a

COLORED LIGHTING has been used throughout the ages to promote well-being. Long associated with a sense of calm and relaxation, blue has been used therapeutically as a form of light therapy.

COLOR KINETICS INCORPORATED   PHOTO: DAN BIBB

Associated with luminous sunshine, the dominant use of **Aspen Gold** elicits an uplifting warmth. Vibrant accents of **American Beauty** red, **Royal Blue,** and light-infused **Afterglow** add exuberant touches to complete this whimsical setting.

Colors, left to right: **Aspen Gold, American Beauty, Blue Iris, Afterglow**

remedy for many illnesses, as a lack of it is a factor in the development of rickets, many bone disorders and vitamin D deficiencies. Sunlight draws people like a magnet, perhaps because of the inherent need for it. It is no wonder that yellow, the color that most symbolizes sunshine, is known as the color of "enlightenment."

Evidently, humans have always been fascinated with the radiating colored light that emanates from fire. Some anthropologists believe that the reason so many people are mesmerized by the incessant lights and color of the television set is because it is a throwback to the time when our earliest ancestors sat around watching the flickering lights and color of fire!

Today there are wellness centers and spas that utilize modern technology by photographing the color of a client's energy field, then applying the complementary balancing color in soothing hydrotherapy baths. Their goal is to marry the best of modern science to the wisdom and traditions of the ancient color therapists.

Archaeological evidence has been cited indicating that in a number of Egyptian temples special rooms were constructed so that the sun's rays filtering in through the windows were broken up into the seven colors of the spectrum. A healer would then diagnose what color the individual required, and he or she would bathe in the room with the appropriate color. This is essentially what some spas offer today, but with more technically attuned equipment and a luxurious bath filled with the appropriately colored water. Having immersed myself (literally) in this experience I can tell you it is fascinating!

Many cultures are aware of the healing properties of color in liquid form. I have worked with Shiseido on a line of body-care products called 5S that celebrates the five senses. The Japanese have always been very sensitive to the importance of color in the stimulation of the senses and how they must all work synergistically to achieve the proper balance in or on the body. They understand that the product must somehow "speak" to the consumer on an emotional level, and the color invariably delivers the message.

Lynn Augstein, of Sausalito, California, specializes in color and light in interiors. She says, "With our hectic schedules and quickened pace we need a place to rest, rejuvenate, and return to our hearts. I achieve interesting dimension by adding colored theatrical gels of specifically selected colors to wash walls and ceilings with radiant transparent color." I followed Lynn's advice and used a blue gel on a rather large loft wall. It is not only restful, but magical as well.

If we believe (as many of us do) that the color of the pigment on walls or the fabrics on furnishings can affect and change our moods, lift our spirits and bring a sense of joy or serenity to us, then we can understand how color in light or liquid form, or many other applications yet undiscovered, may do exactly the same thing.

PHOTO: THIBAULT JEANSON

DESIGNED BY CARL D'AQUINO OF D'AQUINO MONACO INC.

ASK MOST PEOPLE what they see as the color of sunshine, and they will invariably answer "yellow." Varying shades of this happy hue are an instant panacea to dreary days and matching moods.

2 I live in an area where winters are somewhat dreary and the days are short. What can I do to make my home (or office) more cheerful and lift my spirits?

Cheerful is the operative word. Some people literally crave the warmth and cheer that sunlight brings, especially those that suffer from seasonal affective disorder (SAD Syndrome). As yellow is the color that most people associate with sunlight and cheer, I often recommend the use of a warm, golden yellow on the walls such as **Mellow Yellow**, **Custard**, **French Vanilla**, or **Sunshine**.

If yellow doesn't do it for you (and I urge you not to dismiss it until you test it), try a painted surface that simulates a thick, delicious dollop of **Double Cream**. Subtle **Peach** tones will also add a warm, sunny glow and feeling to the atmosphere and help to lift the spirits, just as real sunlight does.

If it is not possible to paint the walls, bring in touches of the above-mentioned colors in posters, paintings, and accessories so that they become a part of your surroundings. If you know a cooperative four-year-old, they will be happy to oblige you with an original painting of the sun complete with radiating spokes all around, as that is often their favorite subject!

Obviously, colors such as variations of red, orange, and yellow are most associated with warmth, so they should become the dominant color choice in your immediate environment.

3 What are color chakras and how are they used?

Some ancient philosophies employ the use of chakras—the seven energy centers in the body that are believed to guide our well-being, energy level, and emotional state. The chakras (from the Sanskrit word meaning wheel) are located at specific points along the body from the top of the head to the base of the spine. These seven centers do not literally exist as physical entities, but simply identify the main colors of the rainbow and the body control points with which they are identified.

In addition, these major chakras are believed to absorb their specifically related color that is then distributed throughout the body. It is also believed that a "free-flow" of all the colors is necessary to maintain physical and emotional well-being, so the intake of colors, often through light therapy, creates a balanced flow within the body.

COLOR CHAKRAS

Although there are some divergent opinions on the color of the crown chakra located at the top of the head, it is generally believed that the following colors represent the influence of each chakra.

Base Chakra: Red
The seat of physical strength, vitality, will, assertiveness, confidence, passion, and ambition

Sacral Chakra: Orange
Governs the ability to be sociable, generous, spontaneous, intuitive, sexual, and to give and accept pleasure

Solar Plexus Chakra: Yellow
The center of self-control, intellect, ego, the second seat of intuition, inquisitiveness, self-esteem, and the ability to be analytical

Heart Chakra: Green
Closely allied to giving and receiving love, security, forgiveness, compassion, balance, cooperation, and self-acceptance

Throat Chakra: Blue
Connected to self-expression, knowledge, communication, truth, trust, and honesty

Brow or Third Eye Chakra: Violet or Purple
Relates to knowledge on an intuitive level, to spirituality, reflection, charisma, and a higher consciousness

Crown Chakra: White (most often)
A knowledge of the infinite, of unity, dedication, and the divine

4 Can some people actually see "auras?"

Throughout the past several centuries, numerous people have claimed the ability to read auras, the luminous radiation of color that they see emanating from the body. In religious depictions a "divine light of energy" is often painted and referred to in religious writings.

In the latter part of the 20th century new credibility was given to the existence of the human aura through a process called "Kirlian photography" developed by two Russian scientists. This specialized kind of photograph records a halo emanating from the body through an electromagnetic energy field. Physical and emotional states may then be ascertained and treated.

Everyone is said to have a major aura color, which fluctuates with mood or state of mind and general health. Many clairvoyants, such as the late Edgar Cayce, were great believers in the existence of a human aura. It is interesting to note that many of the meanings given to colored auras are very similar to the general associations inherent in the psychology of color, as well as those present in ancient philosophies (such as the chakras referred to in the previous question). It certainly indicates that many of our beliefs that are rooted in religion and mysticism often gain greater recognition in later years, especially as technology gives us the tools to learn even more.

While you may not be a believer in things mystical or mysterious, it is always best to keep an open mind. Would our great-great-grandparents have ever believed that colorful living talking images could be moving around in boxes known as television sets or computers? Many of them might have thought of it as "Black Magic!" Our great-great-grandchildren will experience colorful phenomena that we can only imagine.

For those who claim to see auras, there are some divergent opinions on what the color emanations mean. There is, however, a general acknowledgment of the interpretations by various readers. A full range of color means a good state of health, murky or muddy colors mean just the opposite.

Warm Red:	Affection
Deep Red:	Anger
Bright Red:	Sexuality, courage, irritation, egotism
Pink and Rose:	Love of family and devotion
Dull Brown:	Penny-pinching
Gray:	Depression, fear, sorrow, grief
Orange:	Pride, ambition, energy
Red-orange:	Healing, vitalizing
Radiant Yellow:	Intellectual, mental concentration
Pale Yellow:	Illness
Gray-green:	Sly
Bright Green:	Ingenuity, abundance, healing
Pale Green:	Sympathy
Dark Blue:	Integrity, religious belief
Royal Blue:	Honesty, loyalty, deep involvement
Light Blue:	Noble ideas, devotion, healing love
Black:	Hatred, evil, malice
White:	Purifying, uplifting
Red-purple:	Power of the body, worldliness
Violet:	Spiritual

5 What is a "quick fix" for color use in stress reduction?

There is a state of relaxation called the "alpha state" or "alpha rhythm," which is the pattern of electrical activity in the brain when we are awake but relaxed and/or drowsy. Many people are able to control or sustain this alpha state by imagining colorful scenes or using other visual images.

These states can be induced by using meditation and yoga, which in turn can help combat tension and psychosomatic illnesses and achieve a plateau of serenity. One method used is to sit quietly in a room with your eyes fixed on a particular point or imagining a particular colorful fantasy. It could take as long as ten minutes to relax sufficiently; but if you focus on some point in the room, you are less apt to be distracted. The following yoga exercise will help to induce a state of calm:

- Lie flat on your back with knees flexed, relaxing as completely as possible.

- Imagine your consciousness at the tip of your toes.

- Slowly start to draw your consciousness smoothly through your body, beginning with the toes, ankles, legs, arms, and neck.

- Relax the muscles of each area as you slowly draw your consciousness up into your head.

- You should now be totally relaxed and be able to concentrate on an inward image of a deep blue light. Continue to concentrate on that light for three minutes for maximum relaxation.

6 Can "guided imagery" and color be used to change moods?

I know from personal experience that "guided imagery" used in conjunction with color is one of the most effective methods for alleviating stressful situations and inducing happier or calmer thoughts. Just as the name implies, guided imagery is a method of using your own fertile imagination as someone (a practitioner or therapist) takes you on a colorful tour that ultimately banishes tensions and soothes your nerves and changes your mood. Ultimately, you should be able to lead yourself down that same path without assistance. If you don't see yourself as particularly imaginative or fanciful, think again. You have a lifetime of experiences from which to draw.

Similar to the yoga exercise mentioned above, the imagery is best done by relaxing in quiet surroundings where you will not be interrupted. If that means locking yourself in the bathroom and immersing yourself in the tub, all the better. If you are in bed or on the floor, get into a relaxed position, knees flexed. Breathe deeply, slowly, and in a rhythmic pattern as you plumb the depths of your memory for a favorite setting where you have felt truly relaxed, carefree, comfortable, and stress-free. You might have to go back to your childhood to experience these feelings again, or imagine a special place where you have never been but fantasize about being.

Concentrate completely on the fantasy or memory. Recall the scents, listen for the sounds, imagine the shapes, and most importantly, look at the colors.

You might have just disembarked from a cruise ship in the Greek Islands surrounded by incredibly pristine blue water and matching sky, and you are luxuriating in the warmth of the sun and the sparkling white-washed buildings with pots of colorful flowers spilling from the terraces. You can almost smell the fragrant flowers and taste the delicious licorice-like ouzo!!

Perhaps your memory takes you to a magnificent hot pink and purple sunset in Maui. Feel the warm sand between your toes. Or maybe it's a little closer to home (wherever that was when you were a child), to your mother's kitchen filled with the scent of your favorite pie and the color of the red Formica on the countertop (did it have a little boomerang pattern in it!?).

These memories still live deep within your heart and brain because they are stored in your neocortex as millions of neuron impulses, as well as in your amygdala—that portion of your brain that gives emotional meaning to those pungent memories of cooking smells and red Formica.

I wrote quite extensively about guided imagery in *Colors For Your Every Mood*, as I believe that the colors you choose for your physical surroundings can help to shape your moods and inspire wonderful color schemes that can make you feel happier, calmer, more nurtured, romantic, and connected.

7 Can the power of suggestion be used with color as a therapeutic tool?

Absolutely. The answers to the two previous questions are both good examples of the power of suggestion utilizing color. Whether induced by someone else or some other external influence, it is within your own imagination that suggestions must come to fruition. I am a believer, as I have personally seen the benefits of "thinking" in color.

To illustrate my point, as we all know, little fingers love to investigate knobs and locks. When my children were very small they followed me into my bedroom closet and closed the door (after they had turned the knob to the locked position). Not knowing how long it might take for someone to hear us, and feeling the lack of oxygen, I tried very hard to stay calm and composed. But they sensed my panic and started to cry. After calling out to anyone within hearing distance and banging on the door for 15 minutes, my husband, who had been sitting on the patio at the other end of the house, totally absorbed in his newspaper, finally heard us and came to the rescue.

Five minutes later the children had scampered off to play, but I was walking around in a slightly crazed condition with a very sore throat. After that experience, being in an elevator and getting on a plane was a real ordeal. Since my work involves meeting with clients and doing seminars all over the world, my phobia was definitely hampering my life.

I knew that this closet experience probably related to some early childhood event that had really frightened me, but at that point I couldn't remember what it was. I knew it wasn't darkness, as the light was on in the closet. I also knew I needed a quick fix to keep from becoming completely unglued in an uncomfortable situation.

A friend told me about how hypnosis had helped her overcome anxiety. I was somewhat skeptical since I associated hypnotism with altered states, trances, and Las Vegas lounge acts! But I was curious and went to see her therapist. He asked me to describe the problem and then asked whether I visualized the closet experience in black and white or in color. I was really intrigued by this, as I realized my recollection was in black and white—imagine a color consultant thinking in black and white!

PHOTO: DON PAULSON

YOUR OWN FERTILE IMAGINATION can provide an instant form of color therapy. Imagining a colorful image of a special sight, scene, or memory in your mind's eye can help to alleviate a sense of anxiety.

The therapist explained to me that most people see their problems in black and white. As negative recollections, the problems are often thought of as colorless; while positive thoughts, the solutions, should be colorful. He said that black and white thinking places limitations on you and that you can use color as a therapeutic tool to help free yourself from the problem by literally painting it away.

He suggested replacing the uncomfortable, stressful situation in negative black and white with a colorful, comfortable, positive picture. In order for this solution to work at all, you must really concentrate on seeing and feeling the colors. Similar to the imagery mentioned in the previous question, imagine a place where you would like to be. Put yourself in a peaceful garden or on a quiet beach. Think of the surrounding colors. It doesn't make any difference where you are: at your desk, on an elevator, in a plane, or one of the most stressful places—waiting in the dentist's office. Ideally, you would be lying down at home, but the biggest advantage is that your imagination is always with you!

My favorite colorful fantasy is a magnificent sunset. I watch a golden melon-colored ball disappear into the hot purples and mauves of the distant sky, reveling in the dusky blues and the deep teal ocean. I bathe in the silence and the dazzling beauty, breathing deeply and relaxing. I recall a favorite passage about a glorious sunset: "The sky turned the color of pale sherry…the day's last light was like tarnished silver on the bay…."

My anxiety is invariably replaced with a sense of deep relaxation and peace. Every time I find myself in a situation where I am a little concerned about feeling claustrophobic, I paint a gorgeous sunset in my mind. Underground catacombs and caverns are still not my idea of a fun day, but whenever I need a booster shot, I think in Technicolor.

Neurolinguistic programming (that's a mouthful) also uses color suggestion: Subjects are asked to replace a negative word with a positive favorite color word. I am not suggesting that the power of colorful suggestions is the panacea for all problems, but it is certainly worth a try as it won't cost you anything and takes just a moment of your time.

8 Are there specific colors that are recommended for particular health problems?

Certain colors have been used traditionally, both in color therapy as well as in the immediate environment, to alleviate certain conditions. They are:

CONDITION	COLOR CURE
Anxiety	Golden or mellow yellow induces a feeling of optimism, enlightenment.
Claustrophobia	Paint the ceiling sky blue.
Creative "block"	Purple will boost your creativity.
Depression	Vibrant colors lift the spirits.
Depth perception	Yellow lenses in eyeglasses or goggles
Difficulty focusing	Dark blue encourages meditative thinking.
Insomnia	Light, mid-blue, and blue-green induce serenity.
Irritability	Nature's greens are great equalizers and harmonizers. Take a walk in the woods or go to a park. Experience the great outdoors.
Jet lag	Blue and green lenses worn before and during flight
Lackluster love life, lethargy, or fatigue	Red, hot pink, and orange rev up the adrenaline.
Over-stressed	Blues, blue-greens, and greens relax and calm nerves.
Overweight	Avoid vibrant orange, an appetite stimulator, in eating areas.
Underweight	Use orange in eating areas.
SAD Syndrome	Use warm yellows—a ray of sunshine.
Sallow complexion	Wear something rose or pink.
Timidness	Wear black for empowerment (especially with red).
Under the weather	Peach and rosy tones give nurturing TLC.

IMAGE PROVIDED COURTESY OF PANTONE, INC. © PANTONE INC., 2003

9 How can color help to achieve balance in our lives?

Seeking equilibrium is a natural human longing, whether it be physically, spiritually, aesthetically, or emotionally. The ancient Chinese were very aware of this need that they called the balance of yin and yang. In more scientific terms, this balanced state of ease, as opposed to dis-ease, is referred to as homeostasis. Interestingly, these amazing bodies that we inhabit contain a mechanism that always provides an instant visual balance.

For example, if you studied color in school you probably had a teacher who introduced you to a fun and fascinating experiment. Concentrate on any color surface for a few seconds, then look away at another plain surface, preferably white, and you will see what is called the after-image. This is actually the complementary color opposite to the color you were concentrating on. This phenomenon is a graphic example of the body's ability to provide instantaneous restoration of balance through color.

When a cool color is viewed, the after-image will always be a warm color. Conversely a warm color will always be balanced by a cool colored after-image. Although we have no conscious awareness of this colorful balancing act that is going on within us, our eyes will seek out a touch of warming color in a too-cool environment. The sight of the radiating hot flames in the fireplace warms our psyches as well as our bodies. In a room full of warm colors, we welcome the sight and suggestion of refreshing greenery.

Our innate, restorative powers swing into gear when we turn the color temperature up or down. This is especially important in our living and working environments where we are so totally immersed (or not) in color.

The most important point to remember is that one color temperature should be dominant. A room should be approximately 75 percent cool colors and 25 percent warm colors, or vise versa so that a dominant message and comfort level is conveyed: Warm and inviting with a cooling touch or cool and serene with some warm accents. The decision is yours.

If you are really fascinated by the subject of mood and balance, my book titled *Colors For Your Every Mood* explores the subject in greater detail.

10 Can the color of fruit and vegetables be an indicator of their healing powers?

Ongoing research indicates that eating a variety of colorful fruits and vegetables can be extremely beneficial to our optimum health and healing. The color itself is an indicator of its curative powers. For example, eating red and purple fruits has been shown to help prevent heart disease and cancer. There are also non-irritating anti-inflammatory antioxidants in fruits such as cherries, raspberries, strawberries, cranberries, blueberries, blackberries, plums, and grapes. These delicious sources of well-being contain natural dyes called anthocyanins.

THE COLOR OF FRUITS and veggies render vital clues to their health-giving properties. A balanced rainbow of various colored edibles is essential to maximum health.

As we all now know, grape juice or wine (especially red) is considered heart-healthy. Studies have shown that people who drink white wine regularly, but moderately, have stronger lungs than those who do not drink at all. White wine includes compounds such as phenols and flavonoids that reduce oxidative stress, a key element in aging.

Blueberries are the special heroes of the berry family as they also ward off urinary tract infections and the dreaded enemy of all travelers, the "turistas" (known euphemistically in Mexico as "Montezuma's Revenge"). In Sweden it is customary to eat dried blueberry soup to treat troublesome tummy distress. Blueberries have also been shown to improve short-term memory and sharpen reaction time (a good thing at any age)! Along with raspberries, strawberries, and cranberries, blueberries contain vitamin C that is essential to the formation of collagen, so these plump little beauties may also "plump up" our wrinkles.

The lycopene that gives tomatoes, watermelon, pink grapefruit, and guavas their red glow has been shown to be a preventative for prostate cancer. The orange-yellow carotenoids, as they are called, contain the alpha and beta carotene found in carrots, cantaloupes, pumpkins, squashes, and sweet potatoes that help to prevent lung cancer while the cryptoxanthin present in oranges, papayas, and mangoes is believed to decrease the risk of cervical cancer. Interestingly, mangoes contain more fiber (and taste) than a cup of cooked oat bran. Exotic guavas are also high in fiber, and papayas with their rich source of papain work as an excellent digestive.

Melons, such as sweet honeydew and cantaloupe, are high in folates, which help to avert birth defects, and potassium, which lowers blood pressure. Nature's most perfectly packaged fruit, bananas (as well as tomatoes) are another important source of potassium. The custard yellow flesh of the banana contains vitamin B6 as well as magnesium and is believed to help prevent ulcers.

Vitamin A is abundant in peaches, nectarines, and, of course, carrots. But be careful of eating an overzealous amount of these crunchy roots as your skin could turn the same carrot-y color. And it seems that orange juice may be more than just a good way to prevent the sniffles. Recent studies show that the flavonoids in the juice may raise the level of HDL, the "good" cholesterol, while the antioxidants found in the red berry family mentioned above protect against LDL, the "bad" cholesterol, and heart disease. The importance of colorful citrus fruits as a plentiful source of vitamin C has been known for many years, but recent research has shown that additional benefit comes from the cancer-fighting oils in the skin of these zesty fruits.

Those fiery little chili peppers contain capsaicin, the chemical that causes their "heat," while at the same time depletes the substance that transmits pain signals. It can be argued that when the eye-watering heat is turned on, all else is forgotten! Chili peppers have been shown to lessen the itching of psoriasis, the pain caused by shingles or inflammation, as in arthritis. Just adding a sprinkling of hot pepper to soup or soothing broths helps to ease nasal congestion.

The pigment known as lutein, found in spinach, kale, collard, and mustard greens, serves as protection for good eyesight.

As for additional vegetal value, it has long been accepted that there is beneficial nutrition found in everything from red and yellow peppers to purple eggplant, white cauliflower, and green broccoli. So much so, that the American Cancer Society tells us to have five or more servings each of vegetables and fruits a day.

So it seems that your mother's admonition to "eat your veggies" (and fruits) was right on target. But we should add to that advice: For optimal health, eat them in a rainbow of colors.

11 What colors of food are the most appetizing?

We may eat with our mouths, but it is the eyes (and the nose) that lead us to the food. Our noses may lead us to the source of the food, but our eyes make the choices. Only then do our taste buds take over.

The warmer colors of the spectrum are the most visually stimulating and appealing to the appestat, the region of the brain that controls appetite and eating. Reds, red-orange, orange, peach, hot or warm pink, yellows, some red-purples, red lavenders, and yellow greens are the advancing hues that reach out and command our attention.

We see many examples of this in nature. If we observe animals, we can see, for example, the proverbial attraction of hummingbirds to red, bears to golden honey, and monkeys to bananas. For humans and animals alike, the most enticing edible foods are more often in warmer colors, especially in fruits such as red berries, yellow bananas, oranges, and apricots, red apples and yellow apples, and to a lesser extent, yellow-green apples.

Vegetal greens, both light and dark, of course, are important as nourishing foods. But it is the warmer, fresher yellow-greens that hold the most appeal in food. Vegetarians may argue and say all vegetables, no matter what shade of green, are visually appealing appetite stimulants, but even they might have a problem eating turquoise broccoli.

We all know about those tempting temples of the golden arches and the so-called "fast food" warm colors of orange, red, and yellow that are generally used in the interiors of those places. Today the fast food eateries are more often in neighbor-friendly colors, yet the colors of the signage that begs you to indulge remain as warm as the sizzling French fries.

In addition to color, appetizing food must be thought of in terms of how or where it is used. Most people would not think of brown as a particularly appetite-appealing color, unless they see a dark steaming cup of espresso, or view a commercial with someone biting into an incredibly tempting rich fudge brownie with a layer of velvety chocolate icing. Then the appestat is quickly turned on.

THE WARM COLORS, both light and dark, are among the most appetite-appealing. The color of the plates and bowls that hold the food, even in softer shadings, should provide harmonious hues that add to the enticement and stimulate the visual appetite.

PHOTO: ELLEN SILVERMAN, COURTESY OF PFALTZGRAFF

COLOR AND HEALTH

Many mellow yellow and cream-colored foods are perceived as "comfort" foods. Perhaps it re-awakens earliest childhood reactions to applesauce and custards spooned from little jars and other similar baby foods. Interestingly, it was reported that the best-selling foods immediately after 9/11 were comforting childhood-related foods in that same color range: macaroni and cheese, cereals, crackers, popcorn, vanilla ice cream, puddings, custards, and, of course, chicken soup!

White has always suggested purity and refinement, even in foods. However, with the swing to organic and "whole" foods, tans, browns, and warm off-whites, as in whole grain products such as whole grain breads, crackers, cereals, oatmeal cookies, and bran muffins, are favored by many as they suggest earthiness, naturalness, and nutritional advantages.

12 What colors are most associated with luscious and sweet tastes and why?

It's all about pleasure, starting way back in your infancy to your earliest reaction to color and taste, and it is invariably the sweet confectionery colors that are always thought of as not only sweet to the taste buds, but to the eye as well. Think of your first bite of birthday cake with sugary sweet pure white, bubble-gum pink, delicate lavender, lemon-drop yellow, or baby blue icing. Think yellow Necco wafers. Think of a chocolate ice cream cone dripping down on your clean white shirt and leaving a sticky residue gluing your fingers together. Think of hot fudge sundaes with whipped cream and a cherry on top. Recall sugary spun pink cotton candy at the carnival. If you can't remember back that far, observe any baby as it dives to stuff sweet stuff into its little mouth, and you can see that the reaction is almost invariably pure joy.

When you were older, unless you are the rare exception, this translated into more sophisticated tastes, but no less sweet and suggestive of your earliest pleasurable memories. Think smoothies and sherbets, petits fours, delectable fudge ripple ice cream, creamy gelatos, lattes with mocha, and decadent seven-layer chocolate cake. Think blueberry tarts and crème fraise, raspberry glace and banana cream pie. Think strawberry daiquiris and peach melba. Get the picture (and the colors in the picture)?

If you are not already salivating, a look at the "real thing" in the colors mentioned above will immediately elicit the taste of sweet and luscious goodies, just as they did with your first realization that sweet tastes in all of those enticing colors were extremely pleasurable. And it is just these memories that make it so difficult to resist the temptation, especially when there are so many colorful enticements that beckon from the supermarket shelf, the bakery, the restaurant dessert carts, the ads, commercials, and not least of all, the neighborhood Starbucks or Baskin Robbins!

FROM MILKY LIGHT to decadently dark, only the most disciplined dieter could possibly resist the luscious temptation of extravagantly rich chocolate browns.

PHOTO: RICHART CHOCOLATES

13

What colors will help to tempt a balky eater?

If you have a finicky eater you are responsible for, young or old, deliberately use the more colorful foods and combinations of food colors mentioned in the two answers above. If some of those foods are off-limits, use the colors in place mats, tablecloths, dinnerware, and other backgrounds. Use a variety of different colors rather than the same look in colors all the time. This will stimulate attention, add an element of fun, and garnish the visual appetite.

The food may have to be bland for those on a limited diet, but the background needn't be. A beautifully set table or a fun color combination can tempt the pickiest or least enthusiastic eaters.

Of course, there are other methods that might work. One of my friends told me that he was a painfully thin child who had to be coaxed into eating breakfast. His mother tempted him into eating nourishing foods by placing a Hershey's chocolate kiss in the bottom of his cereal bowl. He would dive in to get down to the chocolate treat every time. He truly believes that he ultimately became a confirmed chocoholic as a result of the reward that he kept feeding himself as a much pudgier adult!

14 What colors will make me eat less?

There is a nasty rumor (nasty because it doesn't work!) that blue depresses the appetite. I have never found a group of studies that verifies that so-called fact. As a matter of fact, blue is the most popular color for tabletop china worldwide. So if it followed that blue depressed the appetite and a lot of people eat food on blue plates, it is reasonable to believe that there would be a lot of thin people not concerned about going on a diet. Obviously, it's just not so.

At one point in time it was believed that people simply could not adapt to blue foods as, it was stated, there was no blue food. But, as every Frenchman knows, there has always been blue cheese, and although blueberries are somewhat more purplish than bluish, when blueberry ice cream and yogurt were introduced, consumers became more familiar

PHOTO: BEA STONE

NO MATTER HOW OBNOXIOUS a blue-coated tongue and matching teeth might be to an adult, kids absolutely cannot resist bizarre colors in food, especially if it is sugary-sweet.

with blue-tinged foods. Then came blue corn chips, blue potatoes, and ultimately blue M&Ms and other blue goodies, so that the barrier to blue food has broken down.

It's the kids who really love blue food. They love the shock value of sticking out a bright electric blue tongue and getting an adult reaction like: "That is the most disgusting thing I have ever seen." It's the parents and grandparents who have the most negative reaction, as they were raised in a time when there really was little, if any, blue food.

15 What colors are the biggest "turnoffs" in food?

The colors that still get the most negative reactions are gray, black, and vivid chartreuse-like greens. These shades are rarely, if ever, found in natural foodstuffs, so the eye and the brain find it difficult to connect and associate them with anything appetizing. With the exception of three very distinct tastes, caviar (and how many people have really experienced the taste?), olives, and licorice, black is not very palatable because of the association with decay. Gray is also particularly obnoxious because of the association with mold and decay. In food, it is seen as tainted and definitely not fresh.

The color group that is seen as especially nauseating is the strong chartreuse yellow-greens that are sometimes described as "squished caterpillar" (or worse—I will leave it to your vivid imagination!). The human mind often associates that color with everything slimy, oozy, rotting, and sickly—not a good thing in food. For obvious reasons, hospitals, airplanes, ship interiors, and restaurants should avoid the color at all costs!

Again, kids love the negative reactions they get from adults for certain colors. Calling a neon yellow-green "slime green" is definitely cool to a kid.

Color used out of context can be a real shocker in food or drink. We are so conditioned to an expectation of food being a certain color that our brain finds it difficult, even impossible, to make the transition to an unexpected color. Think of a meal composed of bright purple milk, a gray steak and matching salad, pale blue butter, and black applesauce for dessert. The human mind (and eye) would find it very difficult to wrap itself around such a bizarre sight as it simply defies our expectations.

In the first few months of our marriage, my husband and I took turns trying to outdo each other preparing creative breakfasts on Sunday mornings. One particular Sunday, he decided to add a touch of the exotic by scrambling the eggs with a little bit of wine. Red wine is a blue red and you know what happens when you add blue to yellow. My apologies to Dr. Seuss, but my stomach did a slow turn as I looked down at the green eggs. They were actually delicious, but I ate them with my eyes closed.

Acceptable colors in food can also depend on cultural conditioning. The British love their cabbage white, while Americans prefer it tinged to the green side. They also prefer their eggshells brown, while many Americans are hooked on white. In various countries, bananas are preferred in an overly ripe brownish state, while in the U.S. those "blighted" bananas are headed for the garbage can. And in many countries, oranges are not artificially colored and have a decidedly greenish tinge.

16 What are the best colors to use in health-care settings?

The concept of color in the hospital started with the use of green for operating rooms. It was developed by a San Francisco surgeon who recognized that there was a great deal of glare in the O.R. caused by the use of pure white on walls, towels, sheets, and uniforms. Green was chosen as it is the complementary color to red, the color of blood and tissue that doctors and nurses must focus on for long periods of time.

Testing showed that green keeps the surgeon's eyes acute to red and pink, and relieves glare. Green is perceived as cool, a naturally restorative and healing color. It is also the color of the visual after-image to red, providing in this example a natural balance of a cool color (green) to a warm color (red). (See the color wheel on page 3 and color balance page 91) No longer used in the O.R., white has been adapted as the sign of ultra-cleanliness in high-tech industrial applications known as "clean rooms."

What started as a brilliant idea in one area of the hospital, for very good reason, soon spread to many other hospital areas and ultimately to other businesses, schools, and industrial plants, where it was adapted as the standard and much overused "institutional green." Whether it was appropriate or even necessary was not a consideration. Ultimately, except for in the O.R., green was replaced by institutional white or gray.

Fortunately today there is much more thought and planning that goes into building interiors, especially in hospital settings. Many designers and architects understand that it is vitally important to humanize hospitals and clinics, especially in children's areas—to use colors that will help transform these areas into the nurturing and healing centers that they are truly meant to be.

Where color comes from.

IMAGE PROVIDED COURTESY OF PANTONE, INC. © PANTONE INC., 2003

PANTONE®

CHAPTER SIX

Decorating Your Home

Color is one of the

most important elements

in feathering our nests.

MORE THAN EVER, our homes are critically important to our sense of comfort and well-being where we build our own personal nests. The act of decorating our homes is the catalyst that sparks our creativity, providing that special environment that helps us and those who live with us thrive.

Before you start your search for decorating inspiration, make a commitment to color, or brandish a paintbrush, there are some key points to think about, among them:

- Re-thinking and updating basic color concepts
- Looking at color in relation to pattern and texture
- Putting color in the right light
- Overcoming color "angst"
- And, most importantly, creating the best "color moods"

Although there might be many more personalized questions regarding color in interior décor, the following questions are the most frequently asked. More than likely, you have asked at least half, if not all, of them.

PHOTO: MARGE CARSON

1 What colors can I use on the walls that will appear to be neutral, without having to resort to the usual beige and gray?

We look to Mother Nature for the answer to this question, so I will respond with yet another question: What color is most prevalent in nature? The answer is green, of course, and, in fact, this color family offers more nuances, values, tints, and tones than any other. Interestingly, everyone in the floral industry understands that green is a natural neutral as they almost always use some verdant foliage in virtually every floral arrangement and every color family, including purple asters, red tulips, yellow dahlias, pink peonies, orange poppies, and so on.

VARYING SHADES OF GREEN, especially the more subtle shadings, can function as a neutral color in decorating the home. As in the use of any neutral color, a variety of textures, finishes, details, and contrasts should be used to keep the space from becoming visually boring.

Colors, left to right: **Iceberg Green, Green Haze, Golden Green, Cedar Green, Mood Indigo**

The sage greens emit a quiet, understated feel, the blue-greens are fresh and cool, the hunter greens are stately and dramatic, while the lime greens are so tangy you can almost taste them. There are enough options in this vast array of greens to appeal to every taste.

Still, if green doesn't appeal to you and I can't convince you to use it, another option is taupe. It is more complex than beige or gray alone as it is itself a mixture of both of those tones. There are many variations on the shade, from light to dark and with varying undertones. Taupe can have a slightly rose undertone in shades like **Rose Dust** that work well with cool tones of blue, green, and blue-green, or it might be somewhat golden, as in shades like **Warm Taupe** that compliment warmer tones. Taupe, often referred to as greige, can also have a greenish khaki undertone as in shades such as **Putty**. If it is truly difficult to discern either a warm or cool undertone, that means it is the one of the most neutral taupes, such as **Sand or Simply Taupe**, which work with everything. (See crossover colors page 6)

The advantage of using taupe on the walls is this: It is very basic, never "noisy" or aggressive, conveys a sense of permanence and style, and is not subject to the "ins" and "outs" of trend colors. It is the perfect foil as a background color for trendier home accents.

2 Does white on the walls really "go with everything?"

Contrary to conventional wisdom, painting the walls pure white is anything but neutral. Pure whites are dazzling and appear brilliant to the human eye. The only place where pure whites can be used effectively is as background where there are strong visual distractions, such as large pieces of art that capture the eye quickly. And these pieces should be either vibrant primary colors or classic black and white. This makes for a super-dramatic setting where pure white becomes a part of the drama. And there are some people who are devout minimalists who want nothing more than the starkness (and visual glare) of black and pure white.

But in actual life settings, most people do not crave that kind of starkness. For decorating purposes it is best to add a touch of another shade or tint to pure white to create an off-white, such as turning a **Snow White** into a **Whisper White**. Off-whites are much more effective as neutral backgrounds.

Because it is so highly reflective, especially on fabrics with a sheen, **Pristine** white acts as a mirror as it reflects the color used immediately next to it. For example, if you use a repeating orange pattern on a white background, the white will warm up slightly, because the orange is so very warm (it is actually perceived as the hottest of all hues). Bright colors generally appear slightly dulled next to pure white.

Mixing whites doesn't work. Off-whites will look dull and dingy next to pure white. Antique lace curtains will look yellowed and faded next to a pure white shade. Super-sheer white fabrics disclose the color behind them, so they appear less white than a heavier texture. There are also bluish whites and cool greenish whites, but they have to be handled with care as they can get too sterile and glare just as pure white does. Then there are the rosy whites, peachy whites, and creamy whites that are friendlier because of their inherent warmth. Any shade of white reflects into adjacent areas, which makes it excellent to use near darkened spaces.

And finally, if I haven't convinced you yet about caution in using an icy white, please remember that it enlarges any area in which it is used. So when decorating the bed or the body, anything amply upholstered will look even more so in virginal white.

3 I find myself absolutely intimidated by color when it comes to decorating my home. Is there any hope for me?

Could be that you are suffering from chromophobia —a fear of color!! You might not actually be fearful, just so overwhelmed by color choices (especially if you work in retail or any other color-related industry) that when you go home, you want a quiet space without much stimulation. So you may wish to avoid even the slightest decision about what goes with what. And there is certainly nothing wrong with that, if it is your choice to keep it rather bland.

But if you really would enjoy surrounding yourself with some color, then you should plunge right in. There is no 12-step program for chromophobics, but there is a place to start in order to help you find your comfort level. First, ask yourself these questions: What are your very favorite colors? More importantly, what is the mood you are trying to convey in the various rooms of your home? The colors that you choose help to express those moods or themes. Are you a traditionalist? Do you love going to flea markets and antique shops? Are you from New England and were you raised in a house full of antiques? Did you have a happy, secure childhood? If the answer to all of these questions is yes, then you will probably always be drawn to the traditional colors: **Burgundy**, **True Navy**, **Hunter Green**, **Slate** blue, and warm wood tones.

Not everyone is into traditional colors. You might love fun spaces that are best expressed with whimsical touches of vibrant colors, or perhaps have a need for nurturing shades. There are many moods to explore until you find the one the fits you and your psyche. Here comes a shameless plug: In my book, *Colors For Your Every Mood*, the various "emotional color moods" are discussed and explained. It's a good place to start to help you overcome your inertia-causing, but not terminal, color disease.

BEFORE TAKING THAT FINAL STEP and applying paint on the walls, it is important to think about the emotional aspect of color. The colors you choose will create moods and feelings that will have a great impact on you (and your family's) well-being and comfort level.

PHOTO: SUB-ZERO FREEZER CO., INC.

4

Do I really have to paint the interior of my house white so that it will sell faster?

I know that real estate agents sometimes recommend this, but I don't agree that it is necessary in every situation or in every room. Prospective buyers are generally operating in an emotional mode, which means that a house needs to fit the fantasy or mental picture of where and how they want to live. Color helps to paint the picture and tweak the emotions. If the would-be buyers are first-time owners hoping to raise a family, a nursery painted a non-gender specific color such as **Sunshine** yellow will play right into their fertile imaginations.

Most buyers want to put their own personal color choices into a home, but don't have a clue about what colors to use. If a house is painted to fit the personality of the owners, someone will come along who will feel comfortable with those choices. It is a large part of why they are buying the home. Unless the house is badly in need of a paint job, there is simply enough to do without rushing around and whiting-out the walls.

On a very personal note, my experience has been that buyers have bought because of the colors. When we lived in a rather large home in the Pacific Northwest, we painted each bedroom a different color and called them, the "**Peach** Room," the "**Raspberry** Room," the "**Sunshine** Master Bedroom," and so on. A tiny bathroom was painted a **Deep Water** blue, and most everyone (including the realtors) loved this unexpectedly dramatic and reflective color. And when it came time to sell, the colors and the feelings they evoked played heavily into the buyers' decision.

"*Oh, right,*" you're thinking.... "But *you* are a professional color consultant!!" That's true, but if you need help, or some confidence-building support, there are books, magazines, and websites dedicated to helping you, not to mention color consultants in your own neck of the woods who will be happy to encourage and guide you. They are worth every penny you invest in their opinions, and it will be a great color-learning experience as well.

THE BEAUTIFUL mellow-toned cabinetry in this kitchen provides a light sunny touch to the striking contrast of a deeper-toned wall. Even though the walls are painted a neutral taupe, they provide far more drama with the cabinetry than ordinary white walls.

PHOTO: WOOD-MODE CABINETRY

5 How can I be certain that the color on the paint chip will look the same when it is applied to the wall?

For novice painters (as well as veterans) it is always amazing to see a pastel such as light **Candy Pink** turn to **Bubblegum** on the walls. A small sample will rarely be seen as the same color when viewed on a much larger scale, as the color becomes more intense when you are literally surrounded by it. In addition, there are other considerations, such as the color of the surrounding space, particularly ceiling and floor. Most importantly, it is the quality and quantity of light in the space that will make the difference.

It is always best to start with a sample chip that is more subdued than the color you envision in the space. If you are working with a professional painter, colorist, or decorator, or are brave enough to experiment on your own, you can also try modifying the base color with a dollop of its complementary color (See color wheel, page 3). You can also try "dirtying" the color a bit (not a bad thing in painter's parlance) by adding a pinch of a brownish umber shade sold in tubes and bought in a paint or hardware store. Follow the directions on the label. It's fun and will make you feel a bit Claude Monet-ish. If you prefer a grayer shade, you can always add a bit of black. But, experiment first.

Here are some additional guidelines before spackling and tackling the walls:

- Test the color in the actual setting
- Test your color over a white background. This can be done directly on the wall or on a large poster board or masonite measuring at least five feet by five feet.
- Paint two coats of color over the white.
- Move the board around to different areas of the room so that you can see it at every angle.
- Look at the test at different times of the day to see how the color might change in natural light and artificial light.
- If the effects are pleasing, you are ready to roll.

6 Should I decorate my home in the same colors that I choose to wear?

If you are passionately attached to a specific color or colors, then you would probably enjoy painting the world immediately around you in the same colors. But it is not a given that you *must* use those colors, regardless of any advice you might have been given to the contrary.

Colors in the home should create a mood that may or may not coincide with your personal coloring. Your coloring is either a product of your heredity or whatever cosmetic alterations you have chosen to make, such as coloring your hair or wearing colored contact lenses. Individuals of Asian descent might have lustrous black hair, equally dark eyes, and porcelain skin. They would look fabulous in rich, sparkling, and dramatic jewel tones, such as **Emerald** or **Ruby Wine** juxtaposed against **Raven** black. However, that might not work in their living environments, as it could be too stark and theatrical for their tastes. They might prefer subtler, calmer shades such as **Lavender Gray**, **Celestial Blue**, or **Smoke Green** that speak of quiet, contemplative, and relaxing surroundings.

PHOTO: MARGE CARSON

LARGER FURNITURE PIECES are major investments and are not changed frequently. It is doubly important to choose finishes and colors that capture your eye and "speak" to you. You rarely make a mistake on your initial (and often emotional) reaction when you say, "I love those colors!"

As stated in my book, *Colors For Your Every Mood*, color in the home is more about creating a satisfying harmony with your surroundings. I like to think of it as the four "A" words. First, there is a natural "affinity" and "attraction" that you have to certain colors. Used "adroitly" they can create, as the French say, a certain "ambiance." Every color and color family can help you attain the moods that can make you feel energized, happy and alive, or calm, rested, and secure. Color in the home should be more about satisfying emotional needs than matching your eye color.

Revisit the quiz on page 23. Look at the specific answers that you marked as positive responses because you had some particularly positive feelings about that color. Think about the reasons you marked them that way, and you will eventually connect them to some pleasant associations. It may take awhile to remember some of those associations, but it will occur to you in time. And if you *can't* remember the specific reasons it really doesn't matter. The point is, if the color just feels right, then you need to own it. The only person that needs to give you permission is *you*.

7. What can you do to give the illusion of more space in a small apartment or home?

Conventional wisdom has it that light surroundings, such as walls, carpet, and window coverings, open a small space, giving the impression of greater volume. For the most part, that is true. However, the colors needn't be all pastel, light, or white. Midtones and even deeper tones can be used, especially if you have an open floor plan, as seen in many apartments and condos.

If several rooms are visible from the entry area, a thread of color continuity winding through the visible space will create a connecting link from one area to another, and the eye will find a natural pathway or "flow," creating the illusion of more space. The same is true of adjacent areas where one room is visible from the next, such as a kitchen that adjoins the family room, combination living room and dining areas, bedrooms and adjoining baths, entryways and living rooms.

But small is not necessarily a detriment. Small can also say "cozy" or "intimate," although a light background in a small room with a light and airy window treatment (or none at all, provided the scenery is appealing) is best to keep the room from looking too chopped up and disconnected. On the other hand, doing just the opposite by making the color intense or sparkly can dramatize a small dark space, such as a hallway, entry, alcove, or powder room.

Colors that would be overwhelming in rooms where you spend a great deal of time can be energizing and exciting in small doses. In our current house, we have a really tiny powder room that is the deep rich color of a glass of **Dry Rosé**. On the wall are many of my beaded antique evening bags and miniscule mirrors. It is such a fun space and so totally unexpected when the door is opened to reveal this tiny museum. Small spaces are a wonderful place to have a real flight of fancy.

Deep or vivid colors are most effective in a passageway when it leads to a larger, light area—the visual effect is that of a light at the end of a tunnel. If you want to lengthen a short hallway or passage, paint the walls a deeper tone and keep the floor and ceiling light. Place pictures along the wall in frames to match the ceiling or floor color, forming a horizontal pattern that the eye will follow to create more length.

In order to open up a cramped space, lighten the hue on the wall that needs expansion. For example, if a sofa must be placed on a short wall, lighten both the wall behind it and the wall immediately opposite. The two remaining walls may be darkened to a medium or deeper tone. The same technique works for a narrow room by painting the narrow walls lighter than the wider walls.

To make a square room seem less box-like, one wall can be done in a deeper color than the other walls. Monochromatic or neutral colored schemes unify the space in a small room and give it the illusion of greater size. As a general rule, dark or warm walls enclose a room, while light and cool colors open it up. But again, if warm colors are your preference and the room is small, I suggest going for the mood instead of the illusion of size. The room will be "happier," and so will you.

A ceiling will appear higher if it is painted white or a shade lighter than the walls—light colors will also give the best light reflection. To enlarge small windows use the same shadings in the window treatments as on the walls. Blinds and shutters that have built-in vertical and horizontal lines are excellent expanders. Don't use anything too heavy on small windows and allow in as much light as possible. And unless privacy or fading is an issue, keeping the windows uncovered will aid the illusion of space.

In smaller rooms, it is best to keep the woodwork the same color as the walls. Contrasting colors will divide the wall into sections. In larger rooms, or if size is not an issue, woodwork can be used as an interesting focal point. In a dull entry or hallway, brightly colored doors can add some cheer.

If an area seems too cluttered with jutting protrusions, such as alcoves, dormers, bookcases, and window seats, paint both walls and protrusions in a unifying color. But jigs and jags can also become interesting room features. A dark or vibrant alcove can be transformed into a dramatic background for some special object or personal treasure, especially if the background is done in a contrasting color. For someone who loves loft living, pipes, plumbing, and ductwork can become pieces of contemporary art, turning these eyesores into eye catchers. Instead of fighting the obvious, make them a focal point by painting these squiggly shapes a unique or contrasting color.

Regardless of color, metallic, pearlescent, and mirrored surfaces can also add the illusion of space, because they are light-reflective. Striped papers or painted surfaces with contrasting values and/or hues can create height or width in a room. Color placed effectively in a design can also create a rhythmic flow to draw the eye vertically or horizontally and increase the illusion of room size. Large designs and deep, dark colors can make a room appear smaller, while light, solid colors, and smaller designs can make it appear larger. Many wall coverings come with companion fabrics so that windows and walls can be coordinated for a more spacious look. The fabrics may also be used in upholstered pieces or slipcovers to unify the room's design and flow.

8 Are there any general guidelines for the use of color, texture, and pattern?

Color can be greatly affected and altered by texture or finish as a result of light absorption and light reflection. Think of a newly vacuumed soft-pile carpet and how the colors seem to change depending on the direction of the pile or the viewing angle. Shiny surfaces intensify color, while rough weaves deepen color. The same color can appear brighter in polished cotton than it does in rough wool.

Matte or flat surfaces absorb light and appear somewhat darker than glossy, light-reflecting surfaces. Colors appear lighter and more lustrous on smooth surfaces that have sheen. A **Coral** velveteen pillow will seem much brighter than the **Coral** cotton twill loveseat it sits on.

Shiny surfaces often pick up and reflect the surrounding colors. For example, although glass and chrome are generally thought of as cool finishes, a glass and chrome table may pick up and reflect the warm shadings of a **Brick Red** carpet. As a result, metals are more versatile than painted surfaces because of their reflective quality. It is important to think about how surrounding shades will affect the color of the metal.

Some antiqued or matte finished metals reflect very little, if any, of their surroundings. Deep copper tones will pick up little of cool surrounding tones, no matter how cold the colors appear. Interestingly, utilizing the principles of complementary color (See page 3), cool bluish shades will intensify copper because they are opposites on the color wheel.

In the past there were more rigid rules about metallics and the temperature of the room they inhabit. It was a given that cool colors needed cool metallics such as glossy silver, chrome, and platinum, while warm colors included warmer metal surfaces such as brass, copper, bronze, burnished golds, pewter, and antiqued silver. Currently, taking a cue from fashion jewelry, there is a broader use of combined metallics, such as silver and gold or brass and chrome. This is seen in everything from showerheads and faucets to towel bars, picture frames, and other decorative accessories.

Wood paneling, flooring, and furniture can add more pattern to a room. However, just as with other crossover colors in the natural world, such as the blue of the sky and the greens of foliage (See crossover colors on page 6), natural wood finishes do not intrude into an environment. Brown is the color of bark and stems and twigs. The eye is accustomed to the many shades of brown that surround us in nature, so a variety of wood tones will harmonize with many other hues. As a result of this familiarity, the colors of wood function much the same as neutral tones.

CERAMIC VESSEL BY RICHARD COHEN

SHINY SURFACES reflect changing nuances of color. The temperature of the lighting will also affect surface color. Under an incandescent light source, the blackest blacks and the purest whites will appear somewhat warmer.

If patterns are not similar, such as a flame-stitched needlepoint pillow on a floral patterned chair, but contain the same colors, they will work together.

Similar patterns will also work, but are more visually interesting if the scale is different. For example, a large buffalo plaid sofa in a combination of **Smoke Blue** and **Sky Gray** could be used with a small hounds-tooth check chair done in the same colors.

When accessing the "weight" of patterns of any color, patterns will appear heavier than plain fabrics.

The colors of small-patterned fabrics and tweeds tend to blend together to form another color. A closely spaced **True Red** and **Wedgwood** blue viewed from up close can turn into a purpled effect from a few feet away.

A virtually foolproof way to create a color scheme in a room is to "dip into" the existing colors within the major pattern and use those same colors or undertones of those colors throughout the room. Patterned carpeting and area rugs can be a wonderful source as they usually occupy a large amount of visual space.

Always be certain to check the colors under the best possible lighting conditions as well as in the space they will occupy.

Test the color in the actual setting.

Test your color over a white background. This can be done directly on the wall or on a large poster board or masonite measuring at least five feet by five feet.

Paint two coats of color over the white.

Move the board around to different areas of the room so that you can see it at every angle.

Look at the test at different times of the day to see how the color might change in natural light and artificial light.

If the effects are pleasing, you are ready to roll.

9 Does the artwork on the walls have to match the furnishings in a room (or vise versa)?

Some people involved in the business of art (such as art dealers) will tell you that there doesn't need to be any connection at all. Art is art and furnishings are furnishings. But I will give you a completely personal, totally biased opinion and tell you that it doesn't work that way for me. And it won't for you, if you are very color sensitive.

I truly believe, as the result of working with many clients and observing their comfort levels, that some connecting link needs to exist between the art and the furnishings. Every single painting, poster, and objet d'art do not have to match *everything* in the room, but they should blend (a better word than "match") with *something*.

It will give a greater sense of wholeness and connection to do a visual sweep of a room and feel those color connections running throughout, especially if you are going to go for an eclectic mix of different styles. And the disparate styles will work better if there is that color connection.

For example, a traditional Oriental rug with a strong shade of **Claret Red** running throughout the pattern can meld very well with a contemporary abstract painting that contains a similar color. Note again the

FRAMES BY LARSON/JUHL   PHOTO © MICHAEL WEST

COORDINATION OF MOOD, styling, and color is key to comfort levels. Dappled earth tones on the wall, softly burnished picture frames, natural contrasts in the artwork, an antiqued candleholder, and a warm wood patina on the table, bring a sense of quiet harmony to this vignette.

use of *similar* or *blending* color, not necessarily a *matching* color. You will drive yourself to distraction trying to match colors exactly, especially when they are different materials, or substrates as they are called. A wool carpet will rarely be exactly the same color on paper, canvas, or even in another fabric.

Another important point is to get the "mood" right. A delicate, airy pastel painting will simply be out of character in a room full of vibrant colors. Conversely, a vivid abstract advertising poster will look odd and out of context with delicately colored furnishings. They could work with neutral colors such as a light gray or be very dramatic with black, but pastels simply cannot carry that kind of drama and will be totally overwhelmed by surrounding brilliant colors.

If you really feel safe and secure in a neutral environment, then perhaps a lot of color just won't work for you, even if only in touches. That is your prerogative. If **Sepia**-toned photos in wood frames, a **Carob Brown** leather sofa, and a **Warm Taupe** chair with **Doeskin** suede pillows are your idea of a quiet, restful, understated place, then that is what you need to do. But do remember that although the tones may be neutral, they are still a psychological presence. Neutrals do not actually disappear into the woodwork. They are warm or cool, light or dark, shiny or dull and can work magic, just as the more colorful colors can.

10

How do you integrate colors that are not easily changed in a newly purchased home or when moving into a new apartment?

If you have "inherited" permanent installations such as dismally dark den paneling, a bright orange Formica backsplash in the kitchen, or an Army drab living room carpet, then a decision has to be made as to whether or not you can really live with the color. If you are into kitsch or retro looks, the bright orange could be fun. But if you are like most people, if a color turns you off and you are not interested in doing anything too wild or trendy, a more acceptable solution is to get rid of or alter the offending color.

"Oh, no," you might say. "How can I pull out a perfectly good carpet?" My response is that it might be "perfectly good" from a practical standpoint, but if you choose to decorate around a color that you absolutely detest, you might very well spend more money buying additional colors to "go with" the disliked color or finish and then eventually wind up discarding it all. On a more positive note, think about putting the khaki carpet in a play area or a teen's room where they might think it's the coolest color ever. If you don't have a teen, perhaps a friend does.

In decorating a home, very little is permanent. Structural as well as cosmetic changes can be made more easily than you might think. It does take an investment of time, energy, and/or money, but not necessarily a lot of money. You don't have to be depressed with that dingy, dated paneling in the den. It can be re-finished in another wood tone or simply painted over. Cover the knots in the knotty pine with a product that keeps them from bleeding through, then paint it with a light or midtone color and watch the den come alive.

Apartments are more problematic, especially if there is a testy landlord dedicated to white walls or 20-year-old grasscloth in the entry area. No matter how wonderful the location and floor plan might be, if you cannot decorate to suit your comfort level, it will never feel like home.

PHOTO: JOHN G. HOFLAND, LTD.

WHEN THE BUDGET PRECLUDES any expensive alterations in a living space, or the landlord nixes any changes, a solution is to distract attention from the non-changeable colors by using unique accessories that become interesting focal points.

On the other hand, when starting from scratch, as in an apartment with a cooperative landlord or a brand-new home, you begin with a comparatively blank slate. This might seem like a daunting challenge, but the positive aspect of a fresh canvas is that you get to plan literally from the ground up—from carpet to paint or wall coverings and window coverings and most everything else that will "live" in that house. You have complete freedom to develop a color scheme that really reflects you and your family. You simply start with the appropriate mood or theme, and the color will flow quite easily. (See color moods on page 114)

11 How can artificial lighting change the mood of a room and highlight the colors as well?

First, it is most important to understand the temperature of a lighting source. The standard incandescent bulb emits a warm yellowish light and creates a very inviting mood, especially in the evening. Fluorescent lights give off various shades of white—ranging from extremely cool, which can seem very sterile and harsh, to a subtle and warmer pinkish glow. Dimming fluorescent lights will make them seem less bright, but will also make the surroundings seem duller and grayed. Low voltage halogen also emits a crisp cool light that does appear warmer when dimmed.

The light that is closest in effect to sunlight is called full spectrum lighting. With this form of lighting, there is a greater contrast between black and white. Such bulbs contain an element that filters out an overabundance of yellow light in the spectrum, resulting in a very natural white light. These are the lights that are believed to combat Seasonal Affective Disorder (SAD Syndrome), the depression that results from a lack of sunlight.

Light can be directed to specific areas, such as recessed ceiling lights that will dramatize and spotlight spaces below. They can add dimension and intensity to particular objects, such as focusing on a colorful piece of glass sitting on a shelf. Lights aiming upward to the ceiling will help tremendously to create more height and space to a small or cramped area, especially if the ceiling is painted white or another light color.

There is also recessed or surface-mounted lighting that washes a wall, providing diffuse and interesting effects that enhance the colored surface or textures. Decorative lighting, such as spots or pin lighting, will also highlight a niche, or a particular accessory like a ceramic bowl or other objet d'art where the color effect might disappear without a beam of light to capture its nuances.

Task lighting is the more practical localized lighting that beams on specific work surfaces or reading materials such as on a desk, in the kitchen, or at bedside. It has far less overall effect on color as the source is usually hidden to prevent glare and concentrates only on the task.

Literally "painting" a room with colored light is one of the most dramatic of all effects. Colored fluorescent lights trained on white walls will seem almost magical, as will a similar effect of placing colored sleeves on fluorescents or a colored gel on a spotlight and training those lights on white walls.

If the concept of changing the colors of your walls to enhance or change a mood really appeals to you there are more sophisticated lighting systems available such as fiber optics fitted with color wheels and color-altering LEDs (light emitting diodes), which can easily be controlled with touch buttons or knobs.

12

What do you recommend as a solution when two adults sharing the same space have different color preferences?

Most people share their environment with others. If you have a roommate, significant other, spouse, or children living under the same roof, ask them all to take the quiz in Chapter 2 (page 23). If they are all attracted to the same colors, you simply decorate in combinations of the favorites and everybody is happy.

But, as we all know, real life is rarely that simple. Chances are that color preferences will vary within those people who share the same space. What happens if two or more people who live under the same roof prefer different colors for decorating? Who wins out? Sometimes it's the person with the strongest personality and other times it's the person with the greater confidence level for decorating. Men will often defer to women when it comes to decorating because it has traditionally been the woman's role. However, traditional roles are ever evolving, and men truly should have their say in color choices. It is their environment, too, and they should be in sync with the color choices.

If the men in the house spend a lot of time in front of the TV set in the den or media room, then those are obvious places for doing some of their favorite shades. It is not unusual for a den to be done in the so-called masculine colors such as **Captain's Blue** and **Slate Gray**, or the more traditional shades of **Hunter Green** and **Sesame**. Brighter touches can be added, of course, making it a more versatile setting against a practical background for this gathering space for family and friends.

The person who does most of the family cooking should get to choose the kitchen colors. If they are really color-sensitive cooks, they will choose colors that get their creative juices going, and that's not a bad thing in the kitchen. If cooking is more a chore than a pleasure, that's even more reason to make the surroundings more pleasing and/or stimulating by deliberately using delicious shades such as **Almond Cream** and **French Vanilla**.

DESIGNED BY VLADIMIR KAGAN FOR AMERICAN LEATHER

When two people live together and one is passionately drawn to warm colors and the other to cool, they might wind up fighting tooth and nail over every lamp shade and toothbrush holder. However, this is not as difficult a situation as you might think. Remembering the principles of color balance (See page 91) for example, the dominant color in the bedroom could be cool **Cornflower Blue**, while the subordinate shade might be warm **Lamb's Wool**. This would be an effective solution that would keep both partners content.

Another effective, and for some people more pleasing, compromise is to use crossover colors in combinations (See page 6). Since crossovers are nature's most frequently used shades, many people can relate to those hues and feel comfortable with them. For example, **Eggplant** and **Pewter** could be used with **Sky Blue**. Another example would be **Teal** and **Light Taupe** with a touch of **Deep Claret**. Neutral monotones (See page 11) can also be effective for people with differing color tastes, including some interesting contrasts brought into the mix for accent. For example, a mix of neutral greens such as **Elm**, **Eucalyptus**, and **White Asparagus** with a soft warm touch of **Coral Haze**.

13. My spouse tells me to do whatever I like when choosing colors for our home, but always criticizes the results. Any thoughts on how to handle this?

Beware of that significant other who tells you to do whatever you like. The day the furniture arrives, you may hear something like: "Why did you choose that color?" I have heard many women say, "My husband (or significant other) couldn't care less what colors I choose." Unless he is colorblind (in fact a possibility), he will have some sensitivity to color. Even when he defers to you to make the choices, color choices should be mutually agreed upon. If he (or she) sees the possibilities prior to purchasing, he (or she) will feel a part of the process.

I really think that the word association quiz should be used as a means of understanding how others feel about color. At the very least, it can start a dialogue that will help you understand why your partner has such strong reactions (both positive and negative) to specific colors. You might even learn things about his or her background and upbringing that you never knew before.

14. How do you handle opinionated friends, neighbors, sister-in-laws, etc., who disagree with your home-furnishing color choices?

Every time you make a new purchase, especially for the home, there is an opportunity for people who think they are experts to offer their opinion. The question often posed is, "Do you really *like* that color?" If the color is a new direction for you and quite different from your usual safer choices, and your confidence is a bit shaky, a question like that can really cause some self-doubt.

Try to remember that people's opinions tend to be based on their own color preferences. Have you ever shopped with a friend, considered something in a color you weren't really sure of, and heard the friend say, "*I* love that color—*you* have to have it!" That's exactly what they mean. They love that color, and it's probably one of their favorites, so they judge it to be great for everyone else as well.

WHEN TWO PEOPLE SHARE the same space and have the same sense of style, but differing color tastes, one solution is to combine the crossover colors listed on page 7. In the example to the left, there are two crossovers: sunny yellow and neutral taupe accented with pewter accessories.

I wouldn't want to break up a beautiful friendship or start a family feud but, in spite of their relationship with you, it is difficult for most people to be objective about color unless they are trained professionals with enough experience to be truly objective. However, other than professionals, most people can't help but react to color on a subjective level. If you take your friend's advice about the color you're not sure of, chances are that when you get it home you will never feel comfortable with it. You are better off following your own instincts and reinforcing those instincts by shopping with a color fan guide. That way you won't end up with an expensive mistake. If you do shop with someone else, be certain that it is someone with a really objective eye, or someone whose color sense you have admired and would like to emulate.

15 Is it necessary to carry the same color scheme throughout every room?

No, it is not necessary to use the same colors throughout every room, especially those rooms that are not visible from an entry area. Bedrooms are rarely visible from the living room, especially if the doors are kept closed, so you really don't have to be concerned about repeating the same scheme as in the rest of the house. You're not likely to use the same color in a baby's room that you use in your own bedroom, so you can give everyone his or her favorite colors in the bedrooms. If a den or family room is not visible from the living room, it may be done in different colors. Think of the people who inhabit each of the rooms and the mood you are trying to convey in that space.

If you have a rather open floor plan and many rooms are visible from a central point, or you live in a small space or apartment, weaving a color scheme through visible areas brings a bit more cohesion, a natural pathway that keeps the eye moving through and connecting the spaces. This is especially effective in adjoining areas, such as family rooms and kitchens, bedrooms opening into a bathroom, or entryways dovetailing into living rooms.

In open floor plans, or in small apartments or town houses, the ideal solution is to connect your rooms without utilizing the color scheme in exactly the same way. This is more visually interesting, as in reversing the color schemes in progressing from one area to another. For example, a Hawaiian-inspired bedroom scene in colors of **Scallop Shell**, **Beach Sand**, and **Conch Shell** with an accent of **Orchid** could adjoin a master bath done in **Orchid** with lesser amounts of the other colors. Similarly, a living room in dominant tones of **Silver Blue**, **Malachite Green**, and **Tourmaline** with **Maple Sugar** accents could be reversed in the adjoining dining room, making the delicious **Maple Sugar** shade dominant while the others serve as the garnishing shades.

Again, creating a mood is key to color planning. The answer to the next question will tell you something about how to create "color moods."

16 What exactly are color moods and how do they help in decorating interiors?

Key to decorating an interior is a planned concept of the mood you want to create. It does help to simplify the whole decorating process, giving you a theme and a reference point that defines your space and expresses your personality as well as that of everyone else sharing that space. Color is the single most important contribution to establishing a mood.

First, there are the personal moods. Three of these moods are energetic and active. They are called *Whimsical, Dynamic,* and *Sensuous.* As many people prefer a more peaceful, calming atmosphere, especially in today's hectic world, there are five other moods that are more restful. They are called *Nurturing, Contemplative, Romantic, Tranquil,* and *Traditional.*

We have gone far beyond the old concept of decorating every room in the same color scheme. Decorating by mood allows you to choose the moods and the colors that work best to express the feelings you want to get across in any given space.

Do you want the family room to be a happy gathering place for an exuberant, active family? The *Whimsical* mood says fun-loving, free-spirited, and joyful as reflected in paint-box and jelly-bean bright colors. A typical combination would be **Bright Rose**, **Snow White**, and **Blarney** green.

Perhaps the kids are all grown up and you want the family room to express the same happy feel, but you are ready for more sophisticated fun. Jewel-tones of **Ruby Wine**, **Amethyst**, **Star Sapphire** against **Jet Black** and **Star White** sets a more dynamic mood.

ALTHOUGH THIS CHARMING bedroom might very well be in an urban condo, the whimsical wallcovering is the color of warm lobster bisque, while crisp sailboat white and touches of blue in the lighthouse instantly evoke the feeling of a cottage by the sea.

If your tastes lean to the exotic with a den full of art objects gleaned from multicultural themes, then the rich, dominantly warm (or beyond warm to hot) and luxurious color combinations such as **Curry**, **Hot Pink**, and **Indigo** will impart a *Sensuous* mood for a room that is all about glamour and make-believe.

All three of the above-mentioned palettes are not for the fainthearted as they are very definite, definable, and direct with an inherent energy that is unmistakable. The person who lives in any of those rooms has the confidence to make a strong color statement and never apologizes for his or her choices.

The beauty of the color moods concept is that you do have creative choice in decorating, and it is all based on the feelings that inspire the colors. Just as you might decorate a casual family room and a formal living room in a very different way, you do have creative license to change colors throughout the rooms to express different moods. The following color moods describe a more soothing path than those previously listed.

PHOTO: ELLISON BAY, S. A. MAXWELL CO.

DECORATING YOUR HOME

Forever associated with sky and sea, a *Tranquil* mood calls forth the cool blues, blue-greens, greens, quiet lavenders, and neutrals that create a harmonious, peaceful atmosphere. If serenity is what you long for in the bedroom, your retreat from the world (including the family, when necessary!), then these are the colors that will help you replenish both body and mind. A truly tranquil mood would be set with a combination of **Soothing Sea**, **Angel Blue**, **Blue Moon**, **Snow White**, and **Natural**.

The *Nurturing* palette offers soft, warm colors that invite us to sit down, relax, feeling snug and comfortable. These are the tender tints used in subtle combinations that are not simply used in babies' rooms, but are equally meaningful in adult spaces where a sense of caring, security, and, yes, nurturing is expressed in color. A recommended combination: **Bisque**, **Almond Oil**, **Vanilla**, and **Seacrest**.

The palette that always infuses a room with a rich sense of history is *Traditional*. These are the tones that speak of substance and stability, of a link to the past, that give rooms the feeling of permanence and connection. They are the deep or midtone shades with touches of light or nearly bright accents. Just as the names imply, these are the colors that are always 'in,' regardless of trends: **Barn Red**, **Dark Denim**, **English Ivy**, and **Parchment**.

A *Romantic* mood engages you in everything the word romance implies—closely related, intertwined, loving, inviting, and intimate colors, a tasteful take on nostalgia. This palette may be dominantly cool or warm, or a balanced combination of both, but always done with a soft touch. A typical color combination could be **Mellow Rose**, **Hushed Violet**, **Cameo Rose**, **Cameo Blue**, and **Antique White**.

The *Contemplative* mood is all about home as thoughtful sanctuary, but not without some dramatic touches in accents, especially when used in important focal points such as artwork or an elegant Oriental carpet. Neutrals most often supply the background tones, in light, mid or darkened shades, such as **Charcoal Gray**, **Neutral Gray**, **Limestone** with accents of **Royal Purple**, **Directoire Blue**, and **Deep Peacock Blue**.

There are additional inspirational themes that can inspire color moods. Some might be based on natural themes such as a forest, beach, or a gorgeous sunset, while others are based on favorite travel destinations, real or imagined. The most important message to be learned from color moods is that color preference is based on personal feelings. If you learn to look for the subtle (or not so subtle) personal color clues, you will never make mistakes in color choices.

For more information about the concept and emotional meaning of color moods, as well as additional color combinations, please refer to my book, *Colors For Your Every Mood*.

17 Is blue truly the best color for decorating the bedroom?

The reason blue is often recommended for a bedroom is that many blues speak of serenity, quietude, and tranquility—those peaceful suggestions that prepare us for a restful night of sleep (See answer to Question 16 above). All shades of blue, however, do not deliver the same message. As in every color family, there are varying messages based on the value and intensity of the specific shade.

Many light, mid, and deep blues are especially calming, such as:

- **Sky Blue**—the color of the sky on a clear summer day
- **Deep Ultramarine**—the color of silent ocean depths
- **Cerulean** blue—the color that depicts infinity
- **Dream Blue**—the color of blue sheep
- **Stratosphere**—a misted, muted airy blue
- **Soothing Sea**—the clean, pure green blues of a tropical sea
- **Heather**—the pacifying lavender blues
- **Cloud Blue**—the moody blues

The electric blues imply anything but serenity. Just as the name implies, they send an energetic bolt of lightning across a turbulent horizon. They are a jolt of color and a wake-up call.

Of all the blue hues, the periwinkle shades are the happiest, as they lean far to the purple-red side of the family. As a result, they are the most "expansive" and expressive. At first glance, they may seem to have a calming effect, but bubbling beneath the blue is that irrepressible and mischievous undercurrent of red.

If blue is not your favorite color, the blue-greens, such as **Celadon** or **Sea Foam** will create similarly calming moods. Another option is a cool, quiet lavender, such as **Hushed Violet** or a decidedly grayed cast as in **Lavender Aura**.

Bearing in mind the principle of color balance (see page 91), be cautious of overdoing the cool colors as this can create a sterile, overly cool atmosphere that will not help to foster tranquil surroundings. Bring a touch of warmth into the room by adding some **Pastel Yellow** or **Almost Apricot** accents, perhaps in the artwork or in the bed linens and wall coverings.

18 Are there any rules in choosing colors for a newborn's nursery?

Just as in every other area of color choice, there are no hard and fast rules that exist any more about colors in a baby's room. If you are very traditional in your thinking and you choose to know the sex of the baby before the birth, then the decision is made for you and it would be the inevitable blue for boys and pink for girls. But if you don't know its gender and/or you simply want a beautiful surrounding for your new bundle of joy, there are other options that may, in fact, include some pinks and blues or eliminate them entirely. There are also shades of custard yellows, quiet greens, creamy whites, and hushed violets.

Again, I suggest arriving at a color mood (see Question 16, page 114) as most people would agree that, of all the themes, the *Nurturing* mood sets the tone for the kind of quiet, warm, and caring atmosphere needed in an infant's room. If you want the colors to speak of a soft and loving environment (and who wouldn't), then the combinations of dominantly warm tones balanced by some cool tones is perfect. There is also a healthy glow that permeates a room done in these colors.

This is a joyful, yet stressful time, for Mom and Dad, and they will also need a little nurturing when they stumble into the room for the 2 a.m. feeding! So it's not only about baby, but the caretakers as well.

Possibilities for color combinations are **Tender Peach**, **Vanilla Custard**, **Cloud Blue**, **Cameo Green**, and **Marshmallow**. Another would be **Winsome Orchid**, **Creampuff**, **Pale Banana**, **Reed**, and **Papyrus**.

19 What colors are best for kids' rooms?

This really depends on the child. Some little ones have already begun to show a proclivity to certain colors from the moment they pick up their first crayons, and they will let you know what they are. They might have a favorite cartoon, video game, or movie character that connects to a specific color. Some are ripe for re-doing a room in vibrant colors early on, while others are quite content to stay with the softer nursery colors.

More often than not, it is the parents (or doting grandparents) who make the decisions about the colors in a young child's room based on their own fantasies of what a little boy's or girl's room should look like. There is certainly nothing wrong with that if the child is comfortable with those choices, especially if he or she is particularly tuned in to a color.

One of the biggest problems is parents' and grandparents' tendency to fill the room with too much "stuff," especially overly bright and overly stimulating colored stuff. Would you want to wake up in the middle of the night to see garishly colored glow in the dark creatures, fuzzy and otherwise, with luminous green glassy eyes staring at you?

It is really important for children to have input into the color schemes of their rooms. It's a wonderful exercise in creativity and a real confidence booster in their ability to do this. In addition, it really helps to set the stage for their participation in color and design projects when they get older. Many of the most accomplished interior designers I know have told me that as children they were allowed to participate in color choices for their rooms, and it had encouraged them to pursue colorful careers.

When they become teens, there is no question that they literally participate in the choosing of the décor and color. Most teens wouldn't have it any other way. If they choose something that you deem especially bizarre, you can always make the proviso that they get to repaint it when they tire of its weirdness. To use a cliché, it is "their space." Chances are the door will always be closed anyway, so you won't have to look at the unique color combinations too frequently.

Some especially creative teens may surprise you. Try to keep an open mind and not be too critical or fussy, remembering that, just as it is in the rest of the home, color choices are (and should be) very personal.

I recommend that, even with the littlest ones, you start a color-decorating project by having the kids do a collage. This is a fun and easy project, and all that you will need are magazines, newspapers, yarns, fabrics, leaves from the backyard, beach pebbles, color chips—in short, anything that strikes their fancy and expresses the theme and the colors that they really like. They can be glued to poster board in any way that pleases them, and a color story will emerge.

If they don't have a color mood in mind, it may begin to materialize after the process gets started. You can suggest some of the themes that are mentioned in Question 16, page 114. If "whimsical" is a word or concept that is a bit abstract to them, substitute "fun." Every kid understands fun and fun colors. The same may be done for all of the other moods.

There is no right or wrong way to do this imaginative exercise; it is simply an expression of self. It can lead to some interesting discussions and is a wonderful way to communicate non-verbally with your kids. Actually, it is an even better way for them to communicate with you.

DESIGNER: MICHAEL L. WHITE

MANY KIDS REALLY HAVE a wonderful sense of color and style. They know exactly what they like, and their opinions should be considered in decorating their spaces. Allowing them to participate in the process inspires their confidence and creativity.

20 What do you recommend as a color compromise when two kids share the same space?

Most children of any age are very proprietary about personal space. I remember clearly the weekend drives to the beach, or vacation destinations punctuated by the laments of "Mom (or Dad), his finger is on my side of the seat!!"

Color works very well as a territorial marker. For example, the color of the wall behind each headboard can define a space for each child, while the carpet might be a serviceable coordinating neutral or a patterned combination of the two dominant colors. Two different colors of carpet meeting in the middle is not a good idea as it could lead to more wails of, "Dad (or Mom), she's on my side of the carpet again!"

Corner desks, or possibly just the chair seats, solid-colored bedspreads, shelving, and lamps may also be defined as a color marker for each child. This may not be Mom's idea of a perfectly coordinated room, yet this simple color solution can solve the space ownership issue very efficiently.

Again, each child gets to choose a favorite color and mood. The resulting combination might be a bit "different," but isn't that what creativity and individual expression is all about?

PHOTO: CHICO'S RETAIL SERVICES, INC.

CHAPTER SEVEN

Color in the Workplace

Both in dress and office decor, colors can be appropriate for one business and completely inappropriate for another.

THIS CHAPTER COVERS a multitude of color usages for many phases of your professional and volunteer life. The most frequently asked questions are those regarding appropriate colors for a job interview, color as a means of communicating business messages, as well as color in office décor and retail space.

1   What colors should I wear for a job interview?

As is frequently said, you never have a second chance to make a first impression. So, as color is a vital part of that first impression, it is important to get the color right. First, look at the industry that interests you the most and wear colors that are appropriate for that business. For example, a conservative industry such as banking, accounting, or law will pay more attention to an applicant in a conservative power color like **True Navy** or **Charcoal Gray**. You'll simply look more credible in those colors, and that is the message they want to broadcast to clients.

If you are looking for a job in a glamour industry, women can and should wear trendy colors to accent more basic colors like black so you let them know that you are aware of the latest trends. Men can bring interesting trend colors into shirts and ties, or they can look very GQ in all black. What you don't want to do is wear something as unimaginative as a white shirt and solid tie.

Men should avoid dark shirts and ties with dark suits for conservative industries. You'll look like something out of an old Mafioso movie or too fashion-forward for banking, insurance, accounting, and law firms.

If you are one of many applicants, and chances are you will be, try to make yourself memorable by using a conversation piece for color—a piece of jewelry, a scarf, or a really wonderful suggestion of color around the face, as you will be seated and the interviewer will see you only from the waist up. For example, a **True Navy** sweater with a really terrific **Turquoise** color, perhaps in a piece of jewelry, outlining your face. For men it could be an interesting tie that has a touch of color in a memorable pattern.

Avoid colors that are fun for other occasions like sports or vacation wear, but could look tacky or garish in a job interview, such as really brilliant **Lime Fizz** green or **Mega Magenta**. They are likely to remember you, but for the wrong reasons!

As your anxiety level is high on a job interview, you want to wear colors that make you feel confident, and confidence-building colors are those that make you look and feel your best. For that reason, I recommend wearing your signature colors—those colors that repeat, contrast, and/or enhance your personal coloring. For example, if you have ash blonde hair, deep blue eyes, and fair pinkish skin, your best signature colors would be an **Ash** gray suit with a **Royal Blue** turtleneck or shirt. If you wear a small scarf it could include ash tones and deep vibrant blue, both of which are flattering to your hair and eyes. Adding a touch of contrasting rose tone such as **Cameo Pink** would enhance your complexion color (as rose and pink always do, regardless of skin tone). A man could substitute a tie for the scarf in the very same colors. And please don't think of the pink or rose tones as too "girly"—take a look at some of the fabulously fashionable men's ties and shirts today.

(See signature colors on page 56 for more color combinations based on personal coloring.)

2 What are the current "power" colors?

I do agree with the image consultants' view of this question, and that is that dark colors carry authority. Psychologically, they convey an aura of power and strength. At one time, solid black for daytime was considered too somber and was more often associated with undertakers than over-achievers! But today, black sweaters, slacks, and dresses are considered not only powerful, but ultra chic as well. The power colors can always be combined with your signature colors, such as a black outfit with a patterned tie that contains some of your hair, skin, or eye color.

In addition to black, power colors for men are **True Navy**, **Charcoal Gray**, **Taupe Gray**, **Gull Gray**, **Loden Green**, **Deep Taupe**, and the deepest, richest browns, such as **Black Coffee**.

Women have a greater range of colors to use in expressing power. In addition to those colors mentioned above for men, women can wear **Deep Teal**, **Eggplant** (Aubergine), **Raisin**, and variations of wine, such as **Deep Claret** and **Burgundy**.

The lighter neutrals, such as **Sand**, **Beige**, **Light Gray**, **Tan**, **Khaki**, and **Camel** are not quite as powerful as the deeper shades for both sexes, but they are appropriate in summer months in warmer climates. These lighter neutrals also work in heavier weight fabrics for winter (think **Khaki** wool coat as opposed to **Khaki** cotton pants), although you would be hard-pressed to tell a Texan that he couldn't wear his rugged **Rawhide** brown in any season for any purpose!!

Let me offer a cautionary word about fabric. Although linen is popular in summer, I personally feel it's a challenge to look powerful in summer, no matter how conservative or dark the color, in clothing that invariably looks like you slept in it!

3 My office feels more like a prison than an office, as it lacks any outside window and is totally colorless. How can I create the illusion that the space is more open?

I can really commiserate with you. Many employees complain about lackluster surroundings and how uninspiring they can be. The lack of natural light coming into a space can be so depressing, but color can certainly help to create specific illusions in our surroundings. First of all, bring some sunshine into the space by using some yellow, especially in the spot facing your desk. This can be in a painted surface such as the facing wall or, if it is not possible to repaint the wall, in a piece of art or a poster. As mentioned in Chapter 5, Color and Health, yellow is most closely associated in the human mind with sunshine and good cheer, and will make

PHOTO: DESIGN IDEAS

AN EFFECTIVE WAY to change the cold and sometimes dingy, windowless cubicles often found in the workplace is to use a warm friendly color on the walls. Painting the ceiling blue to evoke the sky and bringing touches of the outside world in through greenery and flowers will also help to humanize the space.

the space appear larger and lighter. A mural of a window on the facing wall is also a good idea as this is most suggestive of light coming into the space.

Another interesting method of opening up a cramped space is to use blue on the ceiling (suggestive of the sky, of course), and if you can sponge on some white puffy clouds, all the better. And bring green plants into the space. This greenery will make you feel more connected with the outside world.

If your employer resists the notion of color in the workspace, bring up the issue of increased productivity in an environment that invites an optimistic, creative, pleasant state of mind that can't help but encourage productivity. It's a no-brainer that even a left-brainer (as many managers are) should comprehend. Productivity is a word they understand even if they don't quite get the concept of color to heighten mood, awareness, comfort, and creativity.

(See the answer to Question #7 on page 125 in this chapter)

4 What are the guidelines for casual dress and appropriate colors in the office?

Fashion has come a long way from the rigidly prescribed rules of the past. Women never dreamed of wearing pants to the office, men always wore a white shirt and conservative dark tie, white shoes were worn from Memorial Day to Labor Day, and anyone who broke those rules was a fashion geek!!

Now most women are wearing pants more often than they wear skirts, shirts are worn in all kinds of colors and patterns, collars come in a variety of styles or don't exist at all, and ties are almost an endangered fashion species. We have a new attitude and it's called "fashion freedom."

But all is not well in Fashion Freedomland. As it is in every democracy, some people abuse their privileges. It has gotten so bad that a national magazine ran a cover story begging the question, "Have We Become a Nation of Slobs?," and network television has run pictures of people in some really tacky states of dress (or undress) that are inappropriate for office.

But most upstanding citizens have good intentions and even though they don't want to go back to the days of fashion dictatorship, they are looking for *guidelines* (that's a much more democratic word than *rules*).

PHOTO: COURTESY OF PAUL FREDRICK MENSTYLE

LESS FORMAL DRESS is the rule in many office settings, but a well-coordinated look is still very much an important component in more casual, yet professional looks. A working wardrobe for men should be built around basic colors and styles that are practical, comfortable, appropriate and attractive.

The basic principles of dressing casually and looking professional are (literally) very simple for men. Build a wardrobe around a few basic pieces that you can wear in several different ways, such as khaki pants, a blazer in navy or neutral colors, cotton knit shirts in different colors, a chambray shirt, or cotton shirts in small prints.

Belts and shoes should be in basic colors like black or brown and as a finishing touch, when you feel a dressier or more fun look is in order, add some colorful ties.

When in doubt, think simple, tailored, and classic in style and wear your signature colors (see page 56) for more interesting, personalized looks.

The basic principles of dressing casually and looking professional for women are very similar. Build a wardrobe around a few basic pieces that you can wear in different ways, such as a navy skirt or pants, a jacket in navy or neutral colors, twin sweater sets, cotton knit shirts in colors, and small- to medium-sized prints in pants, skirts, or tops. If it's too short, too bare, too tight (or too baggy), it's too much (or not enough) for the office, no matter how "casual."

Leave the loud, busy prints, oversized jewelry, and short, short skirts for after five, weekends, or vacations. Stockings really look neater in air-conditioned offices, and shoes shouldn't be too open and bare. (For basic guidelines in accessorizing with color, see page 47.)

Again, your signature colors (as explained on page 56) will help to customize or glamorize your look.

5 Is blue denim appropriate in the office?

It depends entirely on the company policy. In many businesses, denim is allowed on at least one day, while in others the dress code is very loose, the business does not rely on any formality at all, and everyone is relaxed about the idea of jeans or other denim apparel.

If you are a denim lover and feel comfortable in denim clothing of all kinds, from jeans to jackets, you really need to find out about the dress code. If you are the casual type who can't tolerate the thought of more standard business attire, then you might need to make this a priority in accepting a job.

Ask the right questions before you go on the job interview. Check out the office before the interview, if possible, to get an accurate picture of what is acceptable. The worst mistake is showing up for the interview in more standard dress and then switching to something too casual for the following workdays. It looks as if you were playing a role at the job interview and being manipulative in getting the job, then deciding to flaunt the rules by wearing whatever pleases you afterward.

If you work in a home office, there is no problem ever, unless you see clients in your office or you venture out to their offices. Then the same guidelines as above apply. People still think that sloppy clothes equal sloppy work—not a good message if you want to keep their business.

GUIDELINES FOR DENIM IN THE OFFICE

- Wear jeans that fit well, nothing too tight, too baggy, too low.

- Professionalize the look by adding a leather belt and leather shoes in black, brown, or burgundy.

- Sweater sets, fitted jackets, or blazers will also dress up the jeans.

- Neatness counts, so the jeans should be clean. Leave the paint-spattered or bleached-spotted jeans at home for after work.

- Don't wear the distressed looks, novelty dye jobs, sparkle, or studs for the office.

- Denim jackets also work with khakis, over a casual dress or skirt.

- Wear the skirt at a length that flatters your leg. Again, too short is too casual and not for the office.

- Darker denims are even more professional, especially if in a suede finish.

6 What color(s) should I wear when doing a presentation?

Naturally, the type of presentation that you are doing, location, and the audience will have a lot to do with the choice. Is it a glamour industry you will be presenting to? Then you will need more glamorous color choices and combinations. A company or group that is into the latest trends (such as show biz or retail clothing manufacturers) will have an expectation that you know what all of the "happening" colors are, and you will lose credibility if you come in wearing a sober **Charcoal Gray**, unless charcoal is the "new black" that season!

If you are a woman and are presenting numbers to a heavy-duty group of budget directors, you don't want to look like the frosting on a birthday cake. The resistance you might get in a fluffy **Sachet Pink** or blazing **Dandelion** yellow suit will be diminished in a darker power color such as **Deep Taupe**. While I deplore the idea that your intelligence would be in question if you wear a color you love and feel good in, it would take the type of audience described above a while to work through the first impression.

The same concept of power colors is equally important to men. However, if your destination is a seminar in Hawaii, you would look pretty silly in a serious dark business suit and a lei, no matter how powerful the color.

As a color consultant, everyone expects that I will deliver a talk in something colorful. My preference is to put an outfit together that consists of my personal signature colors (as discussed in Chapter 3 on page 56). This always presents an attractive coordinated picture appearance-wise—remember the eyes of the audience are trained on you for the length of the presentation. Anything too busy or too blatantly bright can be visually disconcerting and won't do much for the content of your talk. It might help to keep them awake, but they will be slightly cross-eyed and visually tired by the time you have finished.

COLOR IN THE WORKPLACE

125

If I am presenting to a smaller group and we are working with color, I generally steer away from too much vibrant color as it can be a distraction from the colors I am presenting. Designers will often use neutral colors on the walls of their workspaces for that same reason. If you are doing some intense color matching, the best background is a truly **Neutral Gray**—not too warm and not too cool, but somewhere in-between.

Another important tip for presentation preparedness is to travel in something you would not be embarrassed to wear should you land in the destination city and your luggage is still flying around in the not-too-friendly skies of wherever.

I learned this lesson when I was asked to present color trends for a very large Midwestern company. What I did not know was that the CEO was very well known for his impeccable taste, sense of style, and expectation level. I took a nonstop flight, which lessens the chance for lost luggage, flew in the night before, and traveled in something very comfy. It was presentable, but not enough for a presentation, especially for his very critical eye. Naturally, I found this out about him the next morning after I had arrived and was white-knuckling the arrival of my errant luggage. It did arrive, with only minutes to spare. I tore into my bag, dressed in two minutes flat and raced to the meeting. When he did show up an hour late I will never forget the withering question, "Why, Ms. Eiseman, did you choose to wear taupe with an earth red and warm green?" (Well, at least he was into color!). The actual colors were **Warm Taupe**, **Carnelian** red, and a touch of **Sage Green**. I explained that they were among my signature colors and that really got his attention. So much so, that he asked me to recommend his signature colors!

7 Is there a particular wall color that will make me more productive in the office?

This is one of those "magic bullet" questions that people often hope will have a one-size-fits-all answer. The reality is that there is no one definitive color since productivity is a relative term. What is it you need to be more productive in doing? Are you planning the wall color for an assembly room operation and wanting to know what colors will make the employees work faster? The answer is that there is no one answer. There are many variables that come into play, such as:

- How much natural light enters the area and what direction do the windows face? What is the source of the artificial lighting?
- What are the other colors that are present in the area—flooring or carpeting, blinds, chairs, tabletops, etc.?
- What is the color of the widget you are producing, and is there just one color or many colors?
- What is the geographic location as that will affect the light in the space?

As you can see, an objective, professional opinion would be helpful, preferably onsite.

If you are seeking a color for your own office space, then your own personal take on color will come into play. If you are the outdoor lover and get inspired by communing with nature, then your space should be about green and filled with as many green plants as you can manage to squeeze in. Productivity is not about the "formula" color that works every time in every situation. When you seek your own comfort level, use the colors that are suggestive of a theme and utilize them in your workspace. You cannot help but be more productive.

If you have no say in the color choice, then introduce artwork and posters that are evocative of your favorite things/themes/locations into your environment. Put them in a prominent place where you can focus on them while you are working. If a canoe on a calm, clear blue lake is your idea of heaven, then get a paper-weight that looks like it contains that undulating blue lake. Put it next to your computer and every time you need to immerse yourself in the scene, focus on it.

As simplistic as it may seem, your personal comfort level enhances your productivity, and the color surrounding you can help to spur you on.

PHOTO: TAYCO PANELINK LTD.

IF YOUR PERSONAL PREFERENCES and work habits require a quiet, understated space, then neutral tones will work best for you. But do use an occasional flash of color that your eye can migrate to, as it will provide some visual relief and stimulation.

8 How do I keep my color creativity in full gear so that I won't suffer from burnout?

One of the best suggestions I can make is to go back to school. I don't mean getting yet another degree, but taking all of the fun creative classes that you read about in catalogs for continuing education classes. This is time well spent and gives you great new color perspectives by dealing with different materials than you generally use. For example, has gardening or floral arranging always appealed to you, but you have never made the time to pursue those interests?

What about mosaics made from found objects or broken ceramics, quilting, or watercolor painting? How about glass-blowing or jewelry design? As mundane or artsy-craftsy as they may seem, they will make you look at color in an entirely different way, while giving you new perspectives on the juxtaposition of colors. And the best part is, there is no client or boss to judge your work, just your own sense of joy and gratification.

9 What other avenues of inspiration should people in jobs involving color and design be looking at outside their own industry?

It is important not to become too myopic in finding color inspiration. By myopic, I mean staying too close to your own industry to see what others are doing. Look at the broader world of design, often in unexpected places. Think about all design areas—industrial, set design, floral design, cosmetics (especially counter displays in department stores or stores like Sephora), textile design for both home and fashion, giftware, glass design, costume design. This is not just about current trends, but more about the manner in which color is used and/or special effects.

Your eyes have to be open to many aspects of the world of design, and you might often feel that you are on sensory overload, but as a designer, you can handle it. An intrinsic part of your creativity is the ability to pick up on design elements and color usage so that sometimes you feel like you are getting it by osmosis! Keen observation is part of what you do and who you are, but every designer can get "stuck" occasionally, as there are other everyday distractions that can diffuse your focus.

10

Is having "another pair of eyes" available really helpful in making color decisions on color projects?

The answer is yes and no. The positive aspect of having another opinion is just that—it can help to have another opinion when in doubt, to bounce the colors off someone else. Of course, this person must have an excellent sense of color and be as completely open as possible without too many preconceived notions about what colors should and should not be. And that's not always easy to find.

Sometimes it is an advantage to have someone available who does not always feel the same as you do about color or color influences and will come from a completely different perspective. If you have a co-worker or significant other who fits this description, you have an advantage. But the negative part of this solution is that people often judge color strictly from their own personal vantage point. They react subjectively rather than objectively, and that is not a good thing when seeking an honest, unbiased opinion about color.

My best advice is to go with your own instincts. If you have reason to doubt the use of a particular color or color combination and it just doesn't feel right, then regardless of any other opinion, don't use it. You have to feel it is completely right. In the end, it's your call.

11

How should color be used in home office planning?

Unlike planning a corporate office, the best part of planning a home office is the ability to create a really personal space. You don't have to conform to any preconceived plan in choosing colors that express your personality, taste level, and ingenuity. From formal to informal or homey to high tech, the style and color should be chosen according to the desired mood. (See Chapter 6, Question #16).

If you are a true traditionalist, you will find it difficult to enjoy a sleek, contemporary, minimalist office with monochrome colors. Your comfort zone is best defined by typically traditional shades such as **Forest Green**, **Burgundy**, **Insignia Blue**, **Teal**, **Cadet** blue, **Brown Stone**, **Patrician Purple**, **Antique Gold**, and **Light Taupe**.

If you are the person who loves a whimsical mood in home décor, you can have great fun with color in the home office. Everything from colorful staplers to shelving and colorful computer pads or mice is easy to find. This is also the mood that can be done the least expensively. Secondhand office furniture is readily available, and a cheerful coat of paint can work wonders on a dull gray metal desk or old putty-colored filing cabinets.

Interesting nooks and crannies, jutting protrusions, ductwork, slanted dormers in quirky attic rooms or dark basements all lend themselves well to whimsical colors and themes. If your home office is a spare bedroom crying for a makeover, you have a wonderful opportunity to transform it into any mood you desire. The colors can be different from any others in the home as this is a dedicated enclosed workspace that does not have to conform in any way to various other rooms.

If you have theatrical flair, but have no other room in the house to flaunt it, try a dynamically different **Snow White** coupled with a **Stretch Limo** black accented by dramatic jewel tones such as **Star Sapphire**, **Ruby Wine**, or **Peridot**. This infusion of scintillating color could spark some new creative energy into your work.

A tranquil haven of meditative shades such as **Spa Blue**, **Gray Violet**, and **Purple Haze** provide a quiet refuge where your mind can ponder and plan in a way that it never could in a crowded rabbit warren of office cubicles. A small dark den newly redone in the nurturing warmth of **Mellow Yellow**, **Seedling** green, and/or **Silver Birch** might nurture some new thoughts and concepts as well.

Decorating the dedicated home office in a mood that differs from other rooms also defines the difference between work and home, providing a separate world and atmosphere. I have always enjoyed working at home, but my studio is done in a style and color scheme that is completely opposite to the hues in my home. It disconnects me from any distractions at home and really allows me to focus on work. Of course, the very best perk to working at home is the commuting time!

12 Do you have any recommendations for finding interesting color "markers" or organizers for the office?

The obvious source for color organizers and markers are office supply outlets. They are filled with a myriad of colorful file folders, labels, desktop bins, identifying dots, post-it-type notes that can be assigned to various tasks or clients in specific colors. Don't limit yourself to typical office accoutrements from obvious resources. Challenge yourself to finding colorful markers and containers in unexpected places.

PHOTO: DESIGN IDEAS

ASIDE FROM USING color as an organizational element, it is also a visual motivator that can spark your imagination and creativity. In a home office, you are the boss, so you can pull out all of the stops and get as creative as you like with color.

- Art supply stores and catalogs are a veritable treasure trove for finding colorful organizational equipment.

- Housewares stores for mugs, soup bowls, lazy Susans, and lucite holders (for paper clips, CDs, and other necessities)

- Craft stores, for example: colorful felt coverings that will give a designer look to otherwise boring bulletin, display, or presentation boards

- Hardware stores or builder-supply houses (my personal favorites) for a real nuts and bolts approach to organization.

- Think galvanized tubs as waste baskets, color-coded cords for office wiring, garage bins, painted (or not) for storage. It's absolutely inspirational, fun, and inexpensive.

- Toy stores are full of fun stuff like colorform stickies that act as whimsical labeling.

- Swap meets, flea market finds, and estate sales—one of the most elegant paper-clip holders I have ever found was a rose crystal ink well found at the Pasadena Rose Bowl.

13   Can color be a detriment in decorating a home office?

The mixture of too many busily colored patterns can become over-stimulating visually, causing a " flickering" effect that is too disconcerting in a workspace. Wallcoverings, window coverings, and upholstery fabrics should not be so busy and/or colorful that they distract attention, especially around a computer station.

Work surfaces should be light solid colors, preferably in a non-reflective matt finish. Pure white is not recommended as it can create glare that can lead to headaches and eyestrain.

Available space and its placement are most important in choosing colors for a home office. Dedicated space, as mentioned previously, can be any color scheme, but adjoining or exposed space should coordinate with surrounding areas. For example, an overhead loft that juts out over a living room must have a connection to the space below so that it doesn't look like a floating peninsula that is not linked to its surroundings. Similar colors would keep the open space somewhat grounded.

Another example is an open stairway landing that extends into a second floor hallway. A thread of color continuity will keep the entire area visually connected, especially if the flooring, carpeting, or wall color is consistent.

A slanted wall under a staircase is a marvelous way of eking out extra space. Architecturally, this makes for a very interesting design because of the strong diagonal line of the stair. As this workspace is exposed to the adjoining room, it too should coordinate in color to the surroundings. Because of its somewhat quirky shape, there is an opportunity to be more playful in this space, especially in the color of the shelving or accents on the shelves.

COLOR IN THE WORKPLACE

131

14 Are there any guidelines for color usage in a small retail space?

"Small" is relative. Compared to Costco your space might be miniscule, but small does not mean having to limit colors drastically. Conventional wisdom states that retail space of any size should be neutral in order to allow the colors of the merchandise to star. However, light bland walls are not always necessary, if not downright boring. Deeper shades of neutrals, shades like **Moss Gray**, **Woodsmoke**, **Rose Taupe**, and **Pewter**, can add drama and look very stylish, yet offer a subtle background to merchandise.

Featured merchandise can also benefit from placement in contained vignettes—a grouping of similar themes or colors that can benefit from a dramatizing color background. A display of colorless glass objects might seem to almost disappear into a light background, where a vivid **Carmine** red background would immediately bring focus to the display. Remember to use touches of complementary colors to the background color as this will call even more attention to the area. Against this **Carmine** background, a touch of **Mint Green** or **Turquoise** would afford excellent contrasts, and it doesn't have to be present in the merchandise itself. A green plant or some turquoise-colored stones placed in one of the glass objects would immediately draw the consumer's eye to the display

Brighter colors or attractive color contrasts are excellent attention getters in "dead zones" of the store, areas that are not heavily trafficked as they seem to be out of the way of the usual traffic stream. This technique works well, no matter how small or large the store, as an enticement to draw people to obscure spots on the selling floor.

The background walls do not have to be painted every time a display is changed. If a large piece of wallboard is painted in the dramatized color, it can be moved or repainted when a color change is necessary. The wallboard may also be covered with a wallcovering or a colored fabric. The walls may also be bathed with colored lights, a technique that requires even less effort and, in the long run, less expense. (See Chapter 6, Question #11)

Studies show that most people in the U.S. have a tendency to walk to the right in a retail establishment. So if you want to make better use of your space on the left-hand side of the store, deliberately use an attention-getting colorful display that will tempt the customer to navigate to that space. Interestingly, shoppers in Great Britain have a tendency to walk to the left, leading researchers to conclude that these paths might follow driving patterns in both countries.

COLORS SHOULD ALWAYS present an image of your business or service, so the artful and appropriate use of color and design will help to get your professional persona and imagery across to a would-be client or customer.

15

What are the best colors to use in creating fliers and/or business logos, cards, letterheads, and websites?

Just as color expresses moods and themes in homes and clothing, color should express the message you are trying to convey as well as the purpose of the business or service. White paper and black print are always classic, but rather ordinary unless it is accented with color. The following chart is a guideline for the best color families as well as some specific shades in each of the categories.

WHAT COLOR SAYS ABOUT YOUR BUSINESS

If you want to convey the message that you or your business/service is:

Cool, conservative, efficient
Light to mid-tone neutral grays with contrasting darker gray or black; wine print, blue gray with navy print. Suggested color combinations: PANTONE 443 C, PANTONE 424 C, PANTONE Black 6 C, or PANTONE 222 C, PANTONE 655 C, PANTONE 652 C

Warm, approachable
Cream or warm beige with deep brown print. Suggested color combinations: PANTONE 726 C, PANTONE 4695 C

Fashion–oriented, yet subtle and up-scale
Mid-tones and contrasting deep tones, such as mauve and plum or turquoise and grayed green. Suggested color combinations: PANTONE 683 C, PANTONE 5005 C and PANTONE 7475 C, PANTONE 5575 C

Cosmetics-oriented
Flattering skin tones, such as rose, pink, peach and mocha, rich browns and reds. Suggested color combinations: PANTONE 196 C,

PANTONE 197 C, PANTONE 475 C, PANTONE 7520 C, PANTONE 4725 C and PANTONE 7515 C, PANTONE 7427 C, PANTONE 175 C

Stimulating, high energy
Vibrant warm shades, such as red-purples, warm reds, orange-yellow, and yellow-green. Suggested color combinations: PANTONE 249 C, PANTONE 1805 C, PANTONE 122 C, PANTONE 137 C, PANTONE 584 C

Bold, daring, unique:
Deliberately "discordant" or quirky combinations as well as bold, complementary combinations, such as purple and yellow, hot pink and green. Suggested color combinations: PANTONE 526 C, PANTONE 115 C, PANTONE 1915 C, PANTONE 340 C

Artistic and creative
Unusual combinations, but no discord. Creativity is key with interesting, fashionable combinations. Suggested color combinations: PANTONE 4745 C, PANTONE 4715 C, PANTONE 198 C, or PANTONE 2705 C, PANTONE 4505 C, PANTONE 183 C, or PANTONE 465 C, PANTONE 678 C, PANTONE 1205 C, or PANTONE 371 C, PANTONE 659 C, PANTONE 5205 C

A word of caution concerning fliers or letterheads: If they are to be photocopied (with no color) or faxed, test the colors first by reproducing as a photocopy. Some colors do not reproduce well on some (if not all) machines. Yellow is particularly problematic and could disappear entirely from the text or design.

In designing a website, it is always best to view the intended colors while still in the development phase to be certain that the colors are appropriate and as true to the original intention as possible. The same concept of color and mood that applies to printed pieces also applies to websites. Your website is a reflection of you and your business services. It is a form of advertising that can turn people off instantly if the colors are not appropriate to the business or service.

PHOTO: DON PAULSON

CHAPTER EIGHT

Color in the Garden

Play with color in your garden. Gardens are never the same from one season to the next.

WHETHER YOU HAVE ACRES or a single pot to work with, nature offers a universe of colors to "paint" your outdoors beautiful. On that first spring day, when you stand in your garden, awed by nature and contemplating all that might be planted there, the choices can be overwhelming—which flowers, trees, and shrubs to plant; where to put each carefully chosen one; what to do first. This is where color really counts, as an organizing tool, as a mood setter, as a way to be part of nature's grand scheme. Dip your trowel into these questions and answers, and get the "dirt" on how color can help you achieve your personal outdoor space.

1

Should color be my first consideration in planning a garden?

Are there different color principles in a garden than in other design?

For those who love color, your garden is the place to really experiment—without the fear of making expensive mistakes. Unlike the inside of your house, outside you must work with what nature gives you—climate, soil conditions, sunlight and shadow, the bright blue sky above, the natural foliage of your region, and the areas around your garden space, like views and neighbors' gardens. In dry sunny areas, you'll have backdrops of grays and light browns and silver greens to plan with. In more temperate climates, green in all its variations will provide your canvas. As the garden "artist," you'll add the color, form, and texture to make the garden your own.

Before you plan, watch your garden space as it changes with the seasons and the times of day. In gardens, more than interiors, light affects the intensity of the colors, and climate controls what will grow there. Play with color in your garden. Gardens are never the same from one season to the next. They are ever changing and always miracles of growth and time. Enjoy experimenting there. There are no "best" colors for gardens. Nature is the one place where most colors live happily together.

2

Does the color wheel work in gardens too?

No matter how much you love color, planting bright colorful flowers helter-skelter can be jarring and chaotic if they overpower the quieter colors sitting next to them. A brilliant clump of orange Gerbera daisies would be too raucous a neighbor for tender pink tea roses. The color wheel is a good organizing tool for exteriors as well as interiors. As you learned in interior decorating, the wheel is divided into warm colors (yellow, red, and orange; yellow-orange, red-orange, red-violet) and cool colors (blue, green, blue-violet, and blue-green). For information on the color wheel, see Chapter 1, Question #1.

Green is the most versatile of all colors and ever present as background (or foreground) in foliage, grass, and leaves. Green is Mother Nature's ubiquitous neutral.

As you did inside, determine the "mood" you want for your garden before you select the colors. If you want a tranquil, serene, and contemplative place where you can relax, choose cool colors and pastels. If you want a playful and lively garden, go for those colors in the warm hemisphere of the color wheel.

There are other organizing principles of the color wheel that will help you plan.

Monochromatic Combinations

Plan your garden all in one color, varying the shades for interest. This can be tranquil like Vita Sackville-West's famous all-white garden in England or Impressionist artist Monet's pink and white garden in France. Using all bright yellows or reds in a monochromatic garden is very dramatic. See more about monochromatic gardens later in this chapter in Question 5.

Analogous or Related Combinations

Use the colors that are next to each other on the color wheel—like blue, blue-violet, and lavender to create a harmonious pathway; red, red-purples, orange, and yellow for a theatrical sweep of warm shadings.

Complementary or Contrasting Combinations

When you plant flowers in opposite colors on the color wheel—like yellow and purple, blue and orange, or red among the deep foliage greens, you'll have an attention-demanding, energetic bed of color. Nobody does complementary colors better than Mother Nature herself. Think of a pansy with vibrant purple petals surrounding a bright yellow center or a brilliant red tulip against its verdant green leaves.

3

What kinds of things do professional garden designers take into consideration when choosing colors for a garden design?

I asked this question of Nancy Ballek MacKinnon, who wrote the book, *The Gardener's Book of Charts, Tables & Lists*. She is a partner in Ballek's Garden Center in East Haddam, Connecticut, which is located on a farm that has been in her family since the 1600s and now raises more than 11,000 different plants. "We are real plant people," she says.

Nancy doesn't wait for her clients to ask her questions. She asks them these three questions before choosing the colors for their garden design.

- What kind of a feeling or mood do you want for your garden?

- What time of day do you plan to spend in the garden?

- What time of day does your garden get the most light?

Mood is very important, she says, because most people want to come home from a busy day to the peace and calm of their garden. She chooses serene blues, pale lavenders, and whites for serenity, with white or gray foliage to tie the colors together in peaceful harmony. To create excitement for their exhibit at the annual East Haddam fair, however, Nancy chooses lots of stimulating warm yellows, reds, and oranges to attract people's attention.

Because light so affects perceptions of color, the time of day when you want to enjoy your garden is key to the colors Nancy chooses. If her client arrives home in late afternoon or early evening, she never plants purples or blues since they fade into shadow at that time of day. Soft pastels, whites, and fragrances are her design elements then. But, if her client sits in the garden to eat lunch when the sun is most intense, she might plant that garden with bright yellows, reds, and oranges that can stand up to the light.

Of course, when your garden receives its most light is also a key to color choice. If your garden has sun most of the day, you'll need those dramatic yellows, reds, and oranges to dance in it. A shady garden demands whites and soft pastels for color among the deep green foliage and dark brown earth. These colors stand out against the shadows and deep greens of the foliage that flourish there.

COLORS IN THE GARDEN evoke moods, just as they do in the home. The spotted surfaces and intensive orange of this glorious daylily bring instant exotica to the garden.

PHOTO: DON PAULSON

COLOR IN THE GARDEN

4 Do specific colors have specific meanings in a garden?

Nancy MacKinnon offers the following "Color Personalities" chart to help you choose colors that set the mood for your garden.

Color Personalities

Flowers are like people. Some are bold and brassy, some quiet and subdued. A great deal of a plant's personality is reflected in the color.

White flowers are universal peacemakers. Colors that normally clash when planted close together can suddenly coexist nicely in the same garden when white is incorporated. A loud-colored garden attains a certain refinement when drifts of white flowers are added. White is the most visible color in the shade garden and will draw the eye to a dark corner. White is the color of choice for twilight and moon gardens. Very often white flowers are blessed with exceptional fragrance. If you can't attract pollinators by intensity of color, you can entice them with scent.

Ivory and *cream* flowers soften hot colors and add warmth to cool garden shade—sort of the perfect buffer plant. They can, however, look dirty against pure white backgrounds and somewhat murky against some shades of orange.

Yellow, *gold*, and *orange* flowers provide a glow in the garden and a nice foil to intense blues and purples. They can, however, clash horribly with lavender and mauve or rose shades. Use yellow to lighten the visual weight of the garden, gold to add a richness, and orange to add a punch.

Peach, *coral*, *apricot*, and *salmon* flowers are designer flowers. There are actually very few hardy perennials that fit this description. Perhaps that is why we get so many requests for these colors. In any case, these are sure to surprise and delight, especially when combined with blue or white flowers. Occasionally they will coexist with and even complement burgundy flowers. With most other colors, however, they are discordant at best.

Red and *scarlet* flowers are the loudest and most prominent players in the garden. They are useful in creating a focal point and demanding attention. Be careful, as their strong personality can clash with other colors.

Burgundy and *crimson* flowers are more subdued but very rich in depth and intensity. Burgundy flowers will disappear in the shade or against dark backgrounds. Their regal richness is best displayed against white walls or fences, or in front of gray or golden foliage.

Deep blue-purple, and *blue* flowers add a coolness to the garden and a sense of serenity. True blue flowers are the perfect complement to oranges and yellows. Look at pictures of Monet's gardens and flower arrangements. Purple can add depth and dimension to a garden with lavender and rose shades. Blue is a confusing color in the horticultural world. Very few flowers would actually be considered blue when held up to an artist's color wheel. Lavender blue, violet, and purple are more common. Even named varieties like Scabiosa Butterfly Blue and Iris Blue King are shades of periwinkle and purple.

Black and *green* are novelty or designer flowers, like Black Hollyhock, German Iris, black-flowered Pennisetum, Purple Spurge, Hellebore, and Lady's Mantle.

[Excerpted with permission from *The Gardener's Book of Charts, Tables & Lists* by Nancy Ballek MacKinnon (Capital Books, 2002)]

5 I'm afraid to use a lot of color. Can I use just one?

Yes. As the late Vita Sackville-West says in her classic *Garden Book*: "Provided one does not run the idea to death, and provided one has enough room it is interesting to make a one-color garden. It is something more than interesting. It is great fun and endlessly amusing as an experiment, capable of perennial improvement, as you take away the things that don't fit in, or that don't satisfy you, and replace them by something you like better."

She planted hers all in different shades of white, among silver, soft green, and green-and-white foliage. Long after this famous gardener's death, people visit her white garden to contemplate its variety and peace. Start with your own favorite color and develop a personal color theme garden, or take your color scheme from a flower you particularly like—a peony or rose, with yellow, and deep green leaves, for instance.

PHOTO: DON PAULSON

THE INSPIRED USE OF A RED shed in a garden full of blazing contrasts makes for a delightful montage of color. And in the winter, when the foliage dies back, the bright red structure is cheering on bleak days or provides a striking contrast on snowy white days.

COLOR IN THE GARDEN

139

6 Should my garden color scheme be affected by other elements in my garden, like the stone wall on one side?

Yes. Your garden should be as lovely to view in the winter as in the summer, and that's where "hardscape" elements like wooden decks, pebbled paths, stone walls, building walls and elements, and other architectural features as well as your evergreen hedges and shrubs, barks on bare deciduous trees and plants are most visible.

But in the summer, the color of these "bones of the garden," though softened by the colors and foliage of perennials, trees, and annuals, is still visible. Their color is the canvas against which you should plan the color scheme for summer.

If you are planting a new bed next to the brick wall of your house, be sure to consider the color of the bricks. Consider whether the bricks are blue-red (cooler) or more terra-cotta, an orange or yellow-red (warmer), when planning. Since green is the complement to red, the colors of the shrubbery and foliage of the plants are another consideration. Greens can soften or intensify the colors you choose and will be there in the winter when the flowers die back.

A neutral weathered gray fence is a good backdrop for the bright warm colors of a vibrant, attention-demanding border, or plant soft pastels and cool blues and purples for a calm and serene border that harmonizes and soothes the spirit.

7 Do men's gardens differ from women's?

Only if the man is partially or totally colorblind and has trouble distinguishing red from green. Nancy MacKinnon planned a garden for two of her clients who were both colorblind and could only see red, not green. She planted zinnias, gladiolus, and other flowers in yellows and oranges with interesting textures in the foliage, like broad leaves and tall dramatic grasses. She planned their garden as if it were a black and white photo.

It would be helpful to get the colorblind person's perspective in planting a "textural" garden as they are generally more "shape and form" aware than people with normal color vision. Many colorblind men would respond well and have some interesting input into a garden of variegated succulents or cacti, especially when they are planted in a rock garden.

8   Are floral bouquets different from gardens for color planning purposes?

Not really. The same color principles hold. Putting flowers together in a floral bouquet, however, is a good way to plan a color scheme for a garden. If you like the way the colors work together in a floral arrangement, you'll probably like it in a garden. Again, consider the colors, space, and surrounding environment where both the arrangement and the flowerbed will be when you use this method to plan a color scheme. Some designers even stick flowers in the ground in a bed they are planning to see if the colors and textures work before putting actual plants there.

9   How does climate affect color? Are there different color schemes for different climates or parts of the country?

In your own garden, the color of a plant can be affected by changes in day length, temperature, the amount of rain that falls, and especially by amending your soil with lime, iron, or mineral supplements. If this can happen in your own garden environment, imagine how different a plant's color might be in an entirely different one. Flowers planted in warm dry climates with brighter light and longer days tend to be much brighter than those in cloudy, rainy places. According to Nancy MacKinnon, soils with more calcium, iron, copper, or zinc produce plants with more brilliant color.

For a natural-looking garden, plant in tune with your climate and the colors you find around you. In dense tropical areas, for instance, use the bright vivid reds and yellows and oranges that complement the dark green foliage and flourish there. In dry hot climates where foliage tends to silvers, grays, and soft greens, pastels like pinks, lemons, and violets seem more natural. John Brookes advises, "Be guided by nature and beware of man's interference."

10   I want a garden of peace. What colors would you recommend?

Plant cool colors—blue, purple, and green; pastels like soft pink, powder blue, lavender, and peach; or whites for a calm, serene, relaxing blend. Analogous and monochromatic color schemes in these colors are most harmonious. These colors are best when viewed close up, or set in a shady cool space. They become washed out in harsh midday sun.

11

I want a bold, adventurous garden. What colors would you recommend?

Go for a medley of complementary blues and yellows or purples and oranges, or a swath of flowers in one primary color (an example would be fuchsias in various sizes from the tiniest miniatures to the larger cascading ballerinas). Make sure your plants have dramatic foliage or are planted in a space with bold architectural features.

12

I have a shady garden. How can I brighten it up?

Shade affects growing conditions as much as shadows affect color. Manipulate shade as you would another color. Plant warm colors like red, yellow, and orange as accents to brighten up your cool shade. White is another dramatic addition to a shady garden. Cool colors are most vivid in the shady spaces. Bright light washes them out. Green is the one color in nature that all colors are in harmony with.

13

I have a sunny garden. What colors are best?

If you plan to use your garden in the heat of the day or want it to stand up to bright sunlight, use reds, purples, yellows, and burgundy to absorb the light and look brilliant in it. Pastels fade but set among deep dense green foliage will offer cool relief from the heat of the sun. And if you won't be there to appreciate your garden until the sun has faded, consider planting flowers and shrubs that stand out in the fading light like soft pinks and roses, whites, creams, soft yellows.

GREEN OFTEN TAKES a back seat in the garden, as it is generally thought of as a backdrop to colored florals. However, the varying tones of the vibrant hostas demonstrate that green, in fact, can take center stage. The brilliant pink azaleas (complements to green) make the hostas even more dramatic.

PHOTO: DON PAULSON

14 What colors should I use to make my small garden seem bigger?

Plant your warm bright colors in front and gradually fade off to softer pastels and deep greens, blues, and purples to make the garden feel larger. Balance your warm plantings with four to five times more cool colors to add space, using the bright colors right outside a window to make a room feel larger. Or use all pastels and cool colors for a harmonious space.

15 What colors should I use to make my large garden appear more friendly?

Plant cool colors in front, warm colors in back. If you have a large space and want elements of both, divide your garden into "rooms" that are separated by space—visual walls like fences, house or garden walls, paths or hedges, and levels. Use either warm or cool colors to stimulate the mood you want in those spaces. Or plant "sweeps" of one primary color to link areas or lead your eye to the view.

16 Are there any colors that clash in a garden? How can I soften plantings that are in place?

If you want a mixture of many colors, don't worry because flower colors blend naturally together in most natural settings, but make sure that you match the intensity of hue. The interplay of warm and cool adds richness and vitality to the color combinations of nature. But don't plant a soft lavender next to a dramatic orange. The lavender will disappear. Keep colors equal. A deep green hedge, stone wall, white picket fence, or red brick path can also provide an organizing backdrop for your bouquet of color. Or use a single connecting or echoing color to organize the riot of colors. If you plant warm and cool together, add some white or pastel colors to soften the effect.

17 I want to plant a garden of perennials in the center of my garden. What colors would be best?

Again, decide what you want that center garden to achieve. Do you want it to attract attention and lead the eye and the visitor out to the view beyond? Then plant flowers in those warm, attention-demanding colors, or in a swath of all one primary in varying shades. If that central garden is to be a quiet refuge, plant plenty of cool colors and pastels, and provide shade with a flowering tree.

THE RICH WARM COLORS of this natural perennial garden lead the eye directly
to the soft blue-green view that lies beyond.

18

I live in a garden apartment. I don't have any garden space, just a deck.
What can I do to make my space part of the larger natural space around me?

Use pots of flowers on your deck (or windowsill if you don't have one) and apply the same principles as
in a large garden: bright warm yellows, reds, and oranges close to draw the eye when the view is not the
best. Plant soft, cool pots of plants when you want to harmonize with your surroundings and make your
deck appear to be part of, or draw attention to, the view.

COLOR IN THE GARDEN

19 Should my garden palette change with the seasons?

In nature colors do change with the seasons, starting out with soft yellows and whites and pinks, and ending with deep autumnal reds, oranges, purples, and burgundies. In winter, at least in temperate climates, the flowers die back and you have the deep greens of evergreens, reds of berries, browns and blacks and grays of bark, and the architectural elements of your garden. Using perennials and annuals, you can harmonize with nature through all the seasons.

20 How can I make my garden feel like it's part of the house?

From the outside looking in, use the planting guidelines discussed in Question #6. Your house is very much a part of the garden and should harmonize with it. There's a reason that turquoise houses in temperate climates don't blend. Remember that your garden, during much of the year, is a vital "room" or wing on your house. It should be part of it.

From the inside out, consider the view, what you see outside your windows. Most people plan their interiors before tackling the garden, and it is certainly easier and less expensive to plant new flowers than to replace costly fabrics and wall coverings. If you have large windows that bring the outside in, pick up colors from your home furnishings and take them out. If, for instance, you have blues and yellows in your dining room and a view of the garden, put some of those colors in the beds outside the windows to lead your eye to the garden beyond.

Nancy MacKinnon planned a burgundy and peach garden for a client whose wallpaper had those colors and who wanted a cutting garden outside the windows of the room. She planned a patio garden and blended burgundy and peach flowers with cooking herbs with different foliage textures in whites, grays, and silvers. Since cool gray is not good with warm soft peach, she planted those herbs near the vibrant burgundies.

Windowsill pots planted in vibrant colors will stop your eye when you don't want your view brought inside or warm the view when it is cold and bleak outside.

THE SOFT PASTEL COLORS of the flowers and foliage that line the walk of this garden lead directly to an expectation of the colors that lie within and make the house and garden one. The wallcoverings and fabrics used inside this charming Victorian cottage mirror the colors in its garden.

PHOTO: DON PAULSON

PHOTO: DON PAULSON

Conclusion

I hope this book has answered many of your questions about color. From our emotional and physical well-being to personal image, from embellishing our homes, workspaces, and gardens, to living in harmony with family and friends, color indeed affects almost every aspect of our lives! And I hope that you have been inspired to put more color into your future for excitement, balance, harmony, or just plain fun.

If, by some chance, I've left out a question you'd like to ask, please contact me through my website, www.colorexpert.com. Maybe your question will appear in my next book! —L.E.

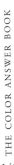

THE PANTONE® SHOPPING COLOR GUIDE

A Portable Color Guide for Matching Color Choices

Pantone, Inc. empowers today's consumer to utilize the language of color in much the same way that professional designers have for the last four decades. With the PANTONE shopping color guide, consumers can now carry with them a portable color guide giving them a more precise way of communicating their color choices and selecting the products in their lives.

Consumers of home and fashion products have a long acquaintance with paint chips, magazine clippings, catalogs, and rug and fabric swatches for coordinating the colors of their prospective purchases. Now, with the PANTONE shopping color guide, customers can bring a portable color memory to their point of purchase. The PANTONE shopping color guide is available through Pantone's website (www.pantone.com).

PANTONE
Color Index

(continued on following page)

149

Credits

AMERICAN LEATHER
(800) 456-9599, ext. 222
www.americanleather.com

BRUCE DALE PHOTOGRAPHY
(703) 241-8297
www.brucedale.com

CARL D'AQUINO
D'Aquino Monaco Inc.
180 Varick Street
New York, NY 10014
(212) 929-9787
www.daquinomonaco.com
monarch@daquinomonaco.com

CHICCO USA, INC.
(877) 4Chicco

CHICO'S RETAIL SERVICES, INC.
www.chicos.com

COLOR KINETICS INCORPORATED
10 Milk Street, Suite 1100
Boston, MA 02108
www.colorkinetics.com

Maximus Spa Lighting:
Intelligent LED
illumination systems by Color
Kinetics Incorporated
Architect: Chris Kofistias
Lighting Therapist: Jovita Wallace

COMFORTAGE INDUSTRIES
880 Lakeside Dr
Gurnee IL 60031
www.comfortage.com

DEBORA HOUSE
Ph: (46) 8 718 0775
www.deborahouse.com

DESIGN IDEAS
Designideas@designid.com

DON PAULSON PHOTOGRAPHY
9875 Miami Beach Road
Seabeck, WA 98380
(360) 830-2212

DYNASTY LANE
(650) 872-8888
www.dynastylane.com

18KARAT
www.eighteenkarat.com

ELLEN SILVERMAN PHOTOGRAPHY
(212) 645-6316

ELLISON BAY COLLECTION
By Piper Designs
A Division of S.A. Maxwell Co.
(847) 932-3700

FIESTA® is a registered trademark of The Homer Laughlin China Company,
Newell, West Virginia
(800) 452-4462
www.homerlaughlin.com

GILD THE LILY
www.gildthelily.com

GRANGE FURNITURE, INC.
200 Lexington Avenue
New York, NY 10016
(800) Grange-1

IDEA ART
Nashville, TN
(800) 433-2278
www.ideaart.com

JOHN G. HOFLAND LTD.
(800) 387-6760
www.hofland.com

LA ROCHÈRE (cover)
70210 Passavant
La Rochère, FRANCE
(33) 3 84 78 61 00

LARSON/JUHL
(800) 886-6126
www.larsonjuhl.com

LLOYD FLANDERS
(800) 526-9894
www.lloydflanders.com

MARGE CARSON
(800) 272-7997
www.margecarson.com

MARLENA BIELINSKA PHOTOGRAPHY
(212) 688-4585

MASLAND CARPETS
PO Box 11467
Mobile, AL 36671
(800) 633-0478
www.maslandcarpets.com

PANTONE, INC.
1-888-Pantone
www.pantone.com

PANTONE VIEW COLOUR PLANNER,
Winter 02/03 edition, published by
Metropolitan Publishing BV,
Amsterdam

RICHARD COHEN CERAMICS
Evanston, IL
(847) 733-9404 or (847) 644-6071

RICHART CHOCOLATES
928A Van Ness Avenue
San Francisco. CA 94109
(415) 351-1800
www.RICHART.com

ROSS-SIMONS
(800) 835-1343

SUB-ZERO FREEZER CO., INC.
(800) 222-7820
www.subzero.com

TAMMY TIRANASAR
(917) 776-0368
www.partially.org/tammytiranasar

VIETRI
(800) 277-5933
www.vietri.com

WOOD-MODE CABINETRY
(570) 374-2711
www.wood-mode.com

Index